SEARCHING FOR AND MAINTAINING PEACE

Visit our web site at
www.albahouse.org
(for orders www.stpauls.us)

or call 1-800-343-2522 (ALBA)
and request current catalog

Searching for and Maintaining Peace

A Small Treatise on Peace of Heart

Rev. Jacques Philippe

Translated by George and Jannic Driscoll

ST PAULS

Originally published in French by Editions des Béatitudes,
Société des Oeuvres Communautaires under the title
Recherche la paix et poursuis-la.

Library of Congress Cataloging-in-Publication Data

Philippe, Jacques.
    [Recherche la paix et poursuis-la. English]
    Searching for and maintaining peace: a small treatise on peace
of heart / Jacques Philippe; translated by George and Jannic Driscoll.
        p. cm.
    Includes bibliographical references.
    ISBN 0-8189-0906-4
    1. Christian life—Catholic authors. 2. Peace of mind—Reli-
gious   aspects—Catholic Church.   I. Title.

    BX2350.3 .P48 2002
    248.8'6—dc21

                                                    2001046073

Produced and designed in the United States of America by the
Fathers and Brothers of the Society of St. Paul,
2187 Victory Boulevard, Staten Island, New York 10314-6603,
as part of their communications apostolate.

ISBN: 10: 0-8189-0906-4
ISBN: 13: 978-0-8189-0906-1

Printing Information:

Current Printing - first digit   10 11 12 13

Year of Current Printing - first year shown

                    2011 2012 2013 2014 2015 2016

Table of Contents

Part Three:
What The Saints Tell Us

Preface

May the peace of Christ reign in your hearts.
(Colossians 3:15)

Experience will show you that peace,
Which fills your soul with charity,
The love of God and of your neighbor,
Is the road that leads directly to eternal life.
(Juan de Bonilla)

Our day and age is one of agitation and inquietude. This tendency, evident in the daily life of our contemporaries, also manifests itself frequently in the domain of Christian and spiritual life. Our search for God, for saintliness, and our efforts to love and serve our neighbors are also frequently fraught with agitation and anxiety instead of being full of confidence and peace, as they should be if we were to find ourselves imbued with the attitude of small children, as the Gospels command us.

However, it is essential for us to come to understand that the way to God and the perfection that is demanded of us is shorter and more efficacious, markedly easier too, when one has learned, little by little, how to conserve, in all circumstances, a profound peace of heart. Because then the heart allows itself to be driven by the Holy Spirit and God is able to do more with it by His grace than the heart could do by its own efforts.

Here then is what we hope to make understood by the considerations presented in the first part of this book. We then review a number of situations in which we frequently find ourselves and try to explain how to confront them in light of the Gospels so as to conserve an interior peace. In the tradition of the Church, this teaching is often addressed by spiritual masters. The third part of the book presents a selection of texts by authors of various ages, who represent and illustrate the different themes that will be alluded to.

Part One

Interior Peace,
The Road To Saintliness

1. Without Me, You Can Do Nothing

In order to understand how fundamental it is for the development of the Christian life to strive to acquire and maintain peace of heart, the first thing of which we must be convinced is that all the good that we can do comes from God and from Him alone: *Apart from Me, you can do nothing,* Jesus said (John 15:5). He did not say, "you can't do much," but, *you can do nothing.* It is essential that we be persuaded of this truth. We often have to experience failures, trials and humiliations, permitted by God, before this truth imposes itself on us, not only on an intellectual level, but as an experience of our entire being. God would spare us, if He could, all these trials, but they are necessary in order that we should be convinced of our complete powerlessness to do good by ourselves. According to the testimony of all the saints, it is indispensable for us to acquire this knowledge. It is, in effect, a necessary prelude to all the great things that God will do in us by the power of His grace. This is why St. Thérèse of Lisieux, the Little Flower, would say that the best thing that God could have done in her soul was "to have shown her her smallness, her powerlessness."

If we take seriously the words cited above

from the Gospel of St. John, then we understand that the fundamental problem of our spiritual life becomes this. How can I let Jesus act in me? How can I permit the grace of God to freely operate in my life?

That at which we should aim is, then, not principally to impose a lot of things on ourselves, as good as they may seem with our own intelligence, according to our projects, etc. Rather, we must try to discover the disposition of our soul, the profound attitude of our heart and the spiritual conditions that permit God to act in us. It is only thus that we can bear fruit — *fruit that will last* (John 15:16).

To the question, "What must we do in order to let the grace of God act freely in our lives?", there is no unequivocal answer, no master key. In order to respond to this question completely, it would be necessary to do an entire treatise of the Christian life in which one would speak of prayer (principally of meditation, which is so fundamental in this regard), of the sacraments, of the purification of our hearts, of docility to the Holy Spirit, and so forth, and of all the ways in which the grace of God could further penetrate us.

In this small work, we do not wish to address all these themes. We simply want to concern ourselves with one element of the response to the question posed above. We chose to speak of it because it is absolutely of fundamental importance. Furthermore, it is too little known and taken into consideration in day-to-day life for most Christians, even those who are very strong in their faith.

The essential truth that we wish to present and develop is the following: To permit the grace of God to act in us and to produce in us (with the cooperation, of course, of our will, our intelligence and our capabilities) all those *good works for which God prepared us beforehand, so that we might lead our lives in the performance of good works* (Ephesians 2:10), it is of the greatest importance that we strive to **acquire and maintain an interior peace,** the peace of our hearts.

In order to understand this, we can use an image (without exaggerating, as we should always avoid doing in making comparisons); but one that can be illuminating. Consider the surface of a lake, above which the sun is shining. If the surface of the lake is peaceful and tranquil, the sun will be reflected in this lake; and the more peaceful the lake, the more perfectly will it be reflected. If, on the contrary, the surface of the lake is agitated, undulating, then the image of the sun can not be reflected in it.

It is a little bit like this with regard to our soul in relationship to God. The more our soul is peaceful and tranquil, the more God is reflected in it, the more His image expresses itself in us, the more His grace acts through us. On the other hand, if our soul is agitated and troubled, the grace of God is able to act only with much greater difficulty. All the good that we can do is a reflection of the Essential

Good, which is God. The more our soul is peaceful, balanced and surrendered, the more this Good communicates itself to us and to others through us. *The Lord gives strength to His people, the Lord blesses His people with peace* Scripture says (Psalm 29:11).

God is a God of peace. He does not speak and does not operate except in peace, not in trouble and agitation. Let us remember the experience of the prophet Elijah of Horeb: God was not in the hurricane, nor the earthquake, nor in the fire, but in the *whisper of a gentle breeze* (cf. 1 Kings 19)!

Often, we cause ourselves to become agitated and disturbed by trying to resolve everything by ourselves, when it would be more efficacious to remain peacefully before the gaze of God and to allow Him to act and work in us with His wisdom and power, which are infinitely superior to ours. *For thus says the Lord God, the Holy One of Israel: By waiting and by calm you shall be saved; in quiet and in trust your strength lies, but you would have none of it* (Isaiah 30:15).

Our discussion is not, it is well understood, an invitation to laziness and inaction. It is an invitation to act, even to act considerably sometimes, but under the impulse of the Holy Spirit, which is a gentle and peaceful spirit. And not in a spirit of disquietude, agitation or excessive hurry, which is too often the case with us. Our zeal, even for God, is often badly illuminated. Saint Vincent de Paul, the last person anyone would ever suspect of being lazy, used to say: "The good that God does is done by God Himself, almost without our being aware of it. It is necessary that we be more inactive than active."

2. Interior Peace and Apostolic Fruitfulness

This search for interior peace could seem quite egotistical to some people. How then can we propose this as one of the principal goals of our efforts, when there is so much suffering and misery in the world?

To this we must first reply that the peace of which we speak is that of the Gospels; it has nothing to do with any type of impassivity, extinction of sensitivity, cold indifference or being wrapped up in oneself, of which the teachings of Buddha or certain tenets of yoga may give us an image. On the contrary, as we will see later, it is the necessary corollary of love, of a true sensitivity to the sufferings of others and of an authentic compassion. Because only this peace of heart truly liberates us from ourselves, increases our sensitivity to others and renders us available to our fellow man.

We should add that only one who possesses this interior peace can efficaciously help his neighbor. How can I communicate this peace to others, if I myself do not have it? How can there be peace in families, in societies, between individual people, if there is no peace first in peoples' hearts?

"Acquire interior peace and a multitude will find its salvation through you," said Saint Seraphim of Sarov. To acquire this interior peace, he strove to live for many years with conversion of heart and incessant prayer. Sixteen years a monk, sixteen years a hermit, then sixteen years enclosed in a cell, he did not begin to bloom visibly until forty-eight years after having given his life to the Lord. But, then, what fruit he produced! Thousands of pilgrims who came to him left comforted, delivered from their doubts and anxieties, enlightened in their vocations and healed in their bodies and souls.

This saying of Saint Seraphim simply gives witness to his own personal experience, which is similar to that of so many other saints. Acquiring and maintaining interior peace, which is impossible without prayer, should consequently be considered a priority for everybody, above all for those who claim to want to do good for their neighbor. Otherwise, more often than not they would simply be communicating their own restlessness and distress.

3. Peace and Spiritual Combat

We must at the same time affirm another truth, which is no less important than that enunciated above. It is that the Christian life is a combat, a war without mercy. Saint Paul, in a letter to the Ephesians, invites us to put on *the armor of God* to fight *not against human enemies… but against the cosmic powers of this dark world and the spiritual forces of evil in the heavens* (Ephesians 6:10-12) and he details all the pieces of armor that we must put on.

Every Christian must be thoroughly convinced that his spiritual life can in no way be viewed as the quiet unfolding of an inconsequential life without any problems; rather it must be viewed as the scene of a constant and sometimes painful battle, which will not end until death — a struggle against evil, temptation and the sin that is in him. This combat is inevitable, but is to be understood as an extremely positive reality, because, as Saint Catherine of Siena says, "without war there is no peace"; without combat there is no victory. And this combat is, correctly viewed, the place of our purification, of our spiritual growth, where we learn to know ourselves in our weakness and to know God in His infinite mercy. This combat is the definitive place of our transfiguration and glorification.

But if the spiritual combat of a Christian is sometimes rough, it is by no means the hopeless struggle of somebody who battles in blindness and solitude, without any certitude as to the result of this confrontation. Rather, it is the combat of one who struggles with the absolute certitude that the victory is already won, because the Lord is resurrected. *Do not weep! Behold the Lion of the tribe of Judah, the Root of David, has been victorious* (Revelation 5:5). He does not fight with his own strength, but with that of the Lord, Who says to him, *My grace is enough for you, for My power manifests itself in your weakness* (2 Corinthians 12:9) and his principal weapon is not a natural firmness of character or human ability, but faith, this total adhesion to Christ which permits him, even in the worst moments, to abandon himself with a blind confidence in the One Who cannot abandon him. *I am able to do everything with the help of the One Who gives me strength* (Philippians 4:13). *Yahweh is my light and my salvation, whom should I fear?* (Psalm 27:1).

The Christian fights, then, against sin, with violence sometimes, called as he is *to keep fighting to the point of death* (Hebrews 12:4), but he fights with a peaceful heart and his struggle is that much more efficacious, because his heart is more peaceful. For, as we have said, it is exactly this interior peace which permits him to fight, not with his own strength, which would be quickly exhausted, but with the strength of God.

4. Peace Is Often at Stake in the Struggle

There is another thing that we must make clear. The believer, throughout the entire battle, whatever the degree of violence, will strive to maintain peace of heart in order to allow the God of Armies to fight for him. Additionally, he must realize that this interior peace is not only a condition for spiritual combat, but is quite often **the goal itself**. Very frequently, spiritual combat consists precisely in this: defending one's peace of heart against the enemy who attempts to steal it from us.

In effect, one of the most common strategies of the devil in his efforts to distance us from God and to slow our spiritual progress is to attempt to cause the loss of our interior peace. Here is what Dom Lorenzo Scupoli, one of the great spiritual masters of the 16th century, who was highly esteemed by Saint Francis de Sales, said: "The devil does his utmost to banish peace from one's heart, because he knows that God abides in peace and it is in peace that He accomplishes great things."

It would be well to keep this in mind, because, quite often in the daily unfolding of our Christian life it happens that we fight the wrong battle, if one may put it that way, because we orient our efforts in the wrong direction. We fight on a terrain where the devil subtly drags us and can vanquish us, instead of fighting on the real battlefield, where, on the contrary, by the grace of God, we are always **certain of victory**. And this is one of the great secrets of spiritual combat — to avoid fighting the wrong battle, to know how to discern, despite the ruses of our adversary, which is the real battlefield, what we truly have to struggle against and where we must place our efforts.

We believe, for example, that to win the spiritual battle we must vanquish all our faults, never succumb to temptation, have no more weaknesses or shortcomings. But on such a terrain we are sure to be vanquished! Because who among us can pretend never to fall? And it is certainly not this that God demands of us, for *He knows of what we are made. He remembers we are dust* (Psalm 103).

On the contrary, the real spiritual battle, rather than the pursuit of invincibility or some other absolute infallibility beyond our capacity, consists principally in learning, without becoming too discouraged, to accept falling occasionally and not to lose our peace of heart if we should happen to do so lamentably, not to become excessively sad regarding our defeats and to know how to rebound from our falls to an even higher level. This is always possible, but on the condition that we not panic and that we continue to maintain our peace.

One could, then, with reason, enunciate this principle: The first goal of spiritual combat, that toward which our efforts must above all else be directed, is **not to always obtain a victory** (over our temptations, our weaknesses, etc.), rather it is to **learn to maintain peace of heart under all circumstances, even in the case of defeat.** It is only in this way that we can pursue the other goal, which is the elimination of our failures, our faults, our imperfections and sins. This is ultimately the victory that we must want and desire, knowing, however, that it is not by our own strength that we will obtain it and, therefore, not pretending that we can obtain it immediately. It is uniquely the grace of God that will obtain the victory for us, whose grace will be the more efficacious and rapid, the more we place maintaining our interior peace and sense of confident abandonment in the hands of our Father in Heaven.

5. The Reasons Why We Lose Our Peace Are Always Bad Reasons

One of the dominant aspects of spiritual combat is the struggle on the plane of thoughts. To struggle often means opposition between those thoughts that originate in our own spirit, or the mentality of our surroundings or even sometimes from the enemy himself (the origin of the thoughts is of little importance) and which cause us disquietude, fear, discouragement and, on the other hand, those thoughts that could comfort us and reestablish our peace. In view of this combat, *happy is the man who has filled his quiver* (Psalm 127) with arrows of good thoughts, that is to say, with solid convictions, based on faith, that nourish one's intelligence and fortify one's heart in times of trial.

Among these *arrows in a hero's hand,* one of the affirmations of faith that should permanently reside in us is that **all the reasons that cause us to lose our sense of peace are bad reasons.**

This conviction is most certainly not founded

on human considerations. It can only be a certitude of faith, founded on the Word of God. It does not reside in the reasoning of the world, as Jesus clearly told us: *Peace I leave with you, My own peace I give to you; a peace the world cannot give, this is My gift to you. Let not your hearts be troubled or afraid...* (John 14:27).

If we seek peace *as the world gives it,* if we expect peace in accordance with the reasoning of the world, or with the motivations that accord with the current mentality that surrounds us (because everything is going well, because we aren't experiencing any annoyances and our desires are completely satisfied, etc.), then it is certain that we will never know peace or that our peace will be extremely fragile and of short duration.

For us believers, the essential reason by virtue of which we can always be at peace does not come from this world. *My kingdom is not of this world* (John 18:36). It comes from trust in the Word of Jesus.

When the Lord affirms that He *gives us peace, that He gives us His peace,* these words are divine words, words which have the same creative force as the words that brought the sky and the earth from the void, they carry the same weight as the words that quieted the storm, the words that healed the sick and brought the dead back to life. Since Jesus tells us, even twice, that He *gives us His peace,* we believe that this peace is never taken away. *God's gifts and His calling are irrevocable* (Romans 11:29). It is we who do not always know how to acquire or preserve them. Because quite often we lack faith.

I have told you these things so that you will have peace in Me. In the world you will have trouble, but take courage! I have conquered the world (John 16:33). In Jesus, we may always abide in peace, because He has conquered the world, because He is resurrected from the dead. By His death, He conquered death, He annihilated the sentence of condemnation that weighs on us. He manifested the benevolence of God toward us. And *with God on our side, who can be against us?... Who could ever separate us from the love of Christ?* (Romans 8:31).

Having discussed this unshakable foundation of faith, we will now examine certain situations in which we frequently more or less lose our peace of heart. We will seek to show, in the light of faith, how vain it is to trouble ourselves in any way.

But first it might be useful to make some remarks regarding those being addressed, for whom the considerations that we will put forth are valid.

6. Goodwill, a Necessary Condition for Peace

The interior peace that we are considering cannot, of course, be shared by all persons independently of their attitude toward God.

Those who oppose God, who more or less

consciously flee from Him, or who flee from certain of His calls or His demands, cannot be at peace. When individuals are close to God, love and desire to serve the Lord, the usual strategy of the devil is to cause them to lose their peace of heart, whereas God, on the contrary, comes to their aid to give them peace. But this rule is reversed for those whose hearts are far from God, who live in indifference and evil. The devil seeks to tranquilize such individuals, to keep them in a false sense of quietude, whereas the Lord, Who desires their salvation and conversion, will trouble and disquiet their consciences in an effort to get them to repent.

One cannot enjoy a profound and durable peace if he is far from God, if his inmost will is not entirely oriented toward Him. "You made us for Yourself, O Lord, and our hearts are restless until they rest in You" (Saint Augustine).

A necessary condition for interior peace, then, is what we might call **goodwill**. We could also call it purity of heart. It is the stable and constant disposition of a person who is determined more than anything to love God, who desires sincerely to prefer in all circumstances the will of God to his own, who does not wish to consciously refuse anything to God. Maybe (and even certainly) in everyday life, his behavior will not be in perfect harmony with this desire, this intention. There would undoubtedly be many imperfections in his effort to accomplish this desire. But he will suffer, he will ask the Lord's pardon for this and seek to correct himself. Following moments of eventual failure, he will strive to come back to his usual disposition of wanting to say "yes" to God in all things, without exception.

Here, then, is what we mean by goodwill. It is not perfection, nor sainthood achieved, because it could well coexist with hesitations, imperfections and even faults. But it is the way, because it is just this habitual disposition of heart (whose foundation is found in the virtues of faith, hope and love), which permits the grace of God to carry us, little by little, toward perfection.

This goodwill, this habitual determination to always say "yes" to God, in the great things as in the small, is a *sine qua non* for interior peace. As long as we have not acquired this determination, a certain uneasiness and sadness will not cease to abide in us — the uneasiness of not loving God as much as He invites us to love Him, and the sadness of still not having given all things to God. Because the man who has given his will to God has, in a certain fashion, already given Him everything. We cannot truly be at peace as long as our hearts have not found their unity and our hearts cannot be unified until all our desires are subordinated to the desire to love God, to please Him and to do His will. This also implies, of course, an habitual determination to detach ourselves from all that is contrary to God. Here, then, is what goodwill consists of, the necessary condition for peace of the soul.

7. Goodwill: Sufficient Condition for Peace

But, conversely, even if, in spite of this, one still has lots of faults and failings, we can affirm that goodwill suffices to be able to maintain one's peace of heart. As the Latin text of the Vulgate says, *Pax hominibus bonae voluntatis* (*Peace on earth to men of goodwill*).

In effect, what does God demand of us, if not this goodwill? What more could He demand of us, He who is a good and compassionate Father, than to see His child desiring to love above all, to suffer if unable to love Him sufficiently and to be disposed, even if he knows he is unable, to detach himself from that which would be contrary to Him. Is it not up to God Himself to intervene at this point and to bring to fulfillment these desires that man, by his own strength, is so powerless to realize completely?

In support of what we have just said, that is to know that goodwill is sufficient to render us agreeable to God, and therefore that we can be at peace, there is an episode in the life of Saint Thérèse of the Child Jesus, reported by her sister Céline:

> "On one occasion, when Sister Thérèse was showing me all of my faults, I was sad and a little upset. I, who so desire to be virtuous, I thought, am so far from it. I would like to be gentle, patient, humble, charitable; Ah! I will never succeed! However, that evening at

prayer I read that Saint Gertrude, in expressing the same desire, had our Lord respond to her: 'In all things and above all else, have goodwill; only this disposition will give your soul the light and the special merit of all the virtues. Whoever has goodwill, the sincere desire to obtain My glory, to be thankful to Me, to share in My suffering, to love Me and serve Me, as well as all creatures, such a person will undoubtedly receive compensations that are worthy of My generosity and his desire will sometimes be more profitable to him than other peoples' good works are to them.'

"Very contented with these good words," Céline continued, "which were all to my advantage, I shared them with our dear little mistress (Thérèse)," who did her one better and added:

"'Have you read what is reported regarding the life of Father Surin? He was performing an exorcism and the demons said to him: "We are able to surmount all difficulties; there is only this bloody dog of goodwill, which we are never able to deal with!" Well, if you don't have virtue, you have a "bloody little dog," which will save you from all perils; console yourself, it will lead you to paradise! Ah! Which is the heart that would not wish to possess virtue! It's what everybody desires. But how few are those who accept to fall, to be weak, who are content to find themselves down and out and have others find them in that condition!'" (*A Memoir of My Sister, St. Thérèse* by Sister Geneviève of the Holy Face [New York: P.J. Kenedy, 1959]).

As we see in this text, Thérèse's concept of perfection (the greatest saint of modern times, according to Pope Pius XI) is not that which we would have spontaneously held. But we will come back to this point. Let us content ourselves for the moment to retain that which concerns goodwill. And let us move on to that which we mentioned earlier, viz., to know how to examine the different reasons which frequently cause us to lose our peace of heart.

Part Two

How To React To That Which Causes Us To Lose Peace

1. The Troubles of Life and the Fear of Being Without

The most common reason for which we could lose our sense of peace is a fear caused by certain situations which touch us personally and in which we feel threatened, apprehensions in the face of present or future difficulties, fear of lacking something important, of not succeeding in such and such a project, and so forth. The examples are infinite and touch all sectors of our lives: health, family and professional life, moral life and the spiritual life itself.

In fact, in each instance, it concerns a good of an extremely variable nature, material goods (money, health, power) or of a moral nature (human capabilities, esteem, the affection of certain people) or of a spiritual nature; goods that we desire or consider necessary and are afraid to lose or not acquire, or which we in fact lack. And the restlessness generated by this lack, or the fear of lacking, causes us to lose our peace.

Faced with such a situation, what, then, could allow us to remain always at peace? Human resources and wisdom, with their precautions, their expectations, their reservations and assurances of all sorts certainly will not suffice. Who can guarantee himself the assured possession of any kind of good, whatever its nature? It is not by making certain calculations and preoccupations that one is going to find a solution. *But who of you can add any time to your life by all his worrying?* (Matthew 6:27). Man is never assured of obtaining anything, and everything which he holds in his hands can easily slip from his grasp from one day to the next; there is no guarantee on which he can count absolutely. And this is certainly not the way that Jesus teaches us. He says, on the contrary, *whoever would save his life will lose it* (Matthew 16:25).

One could even say that the surest way to lose one's peace is precisely to try to assure one's own life solely with the aid of human industry, with personal projects and decisions or by relying on someone else. In what state of anxiety and torment does one place himself who thus seeks to save himself, given our powerlessness, our limited forces, the impossibility of foreseeing so many things and the deceptions that can come from those we count on.

To preserve peace in the midst of the hazards of human existence, we have only one solution: We must rely on God alone, with total trust in Him, as *Your heavenly Father knows what you need* (Matthew 6:32).

> *That is why I am telling you not to worry about your life and what you are to eat, nor about your body and how you are to clothe it. Isn't life*

more than food, and the body more than cloth-
ing? Look at the birds of the sky. They neither sow
nor reap nor gather into barns; yet your heavenly
Father feeds them. Are you not worth much more
than they are? But which of you can add any time
to your life by worrying? And why do you worry
about clothing? Look how the lilies of the field
grow; they neither work nor spin; yet I assure you
that not even Solomon in all his glory was robed
like one of these. But if God so clothes the grass of
the field which is here today and thrown into the
oven tomorrow, will He not clothe you much bet-
ter, O you of little faith? So do not worry, say-
ing, 'What will we eat?' or, 'What will we
drink?' or, 'What will we wear?' It is the Gen-
tiles who set their hearts on all these things. Your
heavenly Father knows you need them. (Matthew 6:25-32).

Evidently, Jesus does not want to forbid us to
do whatever is necessary to earn our food, to clothe
ourselves and to provide for all our other needs. But
He wants to deliver us from the worry that gnaws
away at us and causes us to lose our peace.

Nevertheless, many are shocked by these
words and do not fully welcome them; they are even
scandalized by this manner of viewing things. Still,
what useless suffering and torment they would save
themselves, if they would only take seriously these
words which are God's, and words of love, of con-

solation and of an extraordinary tenderness.

Our great drama is this: Man does not have confidence in God. Hence he looks in every possible place to extricate himself by his own resources and renders himself terribly unhappy in the process rather than abandon himself into the tender and saving hands of his Father in heaven. Yet, how unjustified this lack of confidence is! Isn't it absurd that a child would thus doubt his Father, when this Father is the best and most powerful Who could exist, when He is the Father in heaven? In spite of that, it is in this absurdity that we most frequently live. Listen to the gentle reproach that the Lord addressed to us through the mouth of Saint Catherine of Siena:

> "Why don't you have confidence in me, your creator? Why do you rely on yourself? Am I not faithful and loyal to you? Redeemed and restored to grace by virtue of the blood of my only Son, man can then say that he has experienced my fidelity. And, nevertheless, he still doubts, it would appear, that I am sufficiently powerful to help him, sufficiently strong to help and defend him against his enemies, sufficiently wise to illuminate the eyes of his intelligence or that I have sufficient clemency to want to give him whatever is necessary for his salvation. It would appear that I am not sufficiently rich to make his fortune,

not beautiful enough to make him beautiful; one might say that he is afraid not to find enough bread in my home to nourish himself, nor clothing with which to cover himself." (*The Dialogue of St. Catherine of Siena*, Algar Thorold, tr., TAN Books & Publishers, 1991, chapter 140).

How many young people, for example, hesitate to give their lives entirely to God because they do not have confidence that God is capable of making them completely happy. And they seek to assure their own happiness by themselves and they make themselves sad and unhappy in the process.

This is precisely the great victory of the Father of Lies, of the Accuser: succeeding in putting into the heart of a child of God distrust vis-à-vis his Father!

It is, however, marked with this distrust that we come into this world. This is the *original* sin. And all our spiritual life consists precisely in a long process of reeducation, with a view to regaining that lost confidence, by the grace of the Holy Spirit Who makes us say anew to God: *Abba, Father!*

But it is true that this "return to confidence" is very difficult for us, long and painful. There are two principal obstacles.

2. Our Difficulty in Believing in Providence

The first obstacle is that, as long as we have not experienced concretely the fidelity of Divine Providence to provide for our essential needs, we have difficulty believing in it and we abandon it. We have hard heads, the words of Jesus do not suffice for us, we want to see at least a little in order to believe! Well, we do not see it operating around us in a clear manner. How, then, are we to experience it?

It is important to know one thing: We cannot experience this support from God unless we leave Him the necessary space in which He can express Himself. I would like to make a comparison. As long as a person who must jump with a parachute does not jump out into the void, he cannot feel that the cords of the parachute will support him, because the parachute has not yet had the chance to open. One must first jump and it is only later that one feels carried. And so it is in spiritual life: "God gives in the measure that we expect of Him," says Saint John of the Cross. And Saint Francis de Sales says: "The measure of Divine Providence acting on us is the degree of confidence that we have in it." This is where the problem lies. Many do not believe in Providence because they've never experienced it, but they've never experienced it because they've never jumped into the void and taken the leap of faith. They never give it the possibility to intervene. They calculate everything, anticipate everything, they seek to resolve everything by counting on themselves, instead of counting on God. The founders of religious orders proceed with the audacity of this spirit of faith. They buy houses without having a penny, they receive the poor although they have nothing with which to feed them. Then, God performs miracles for them. The checks arrive and the granaries are filled. But, too often, generations later, everything is planned, calculated. One doesn't incur an expense without being sure in advance to have enough to cover it. How can Providence manifest itself? And the same is true in the spiritual life. If a priest drafts all his sermons and his talks, down to the least comma, in order to be sure that he does not find himself wanting before his audience, and never has the audacity to begin preaching with a prayer and confidence in God as his only preparation, how can he have this beautiful experience of the Holy Spirit, Who speaks through his mouth? Does the Gospel not say, ...*do not worry about how to speak or what you should say; for what you are to say will be given to you when the time comes; because it will not be you who will be speaking, but the Spirit of your Father will be speaking in you* (Matthew 10:19)?

Let us be very clear. Obviously we do not want to say that it is a bad thing to be able to anticipate things, to develop a budget or prepare one's homilies. Our natural abilities are also instruments in the hands of Providence! But everything depends on the spirit in which we do things. We must clearly understand that there is an enormous difference in attitude of heart between one, who in fear of finding himself wanting because he does not believe in the intervention of God on behalf of those who lean on Him, programs everything in advance to the smallest detail and does not undertake anything except in the exact measure of its actual possibilities, and one who certainly undertakes legitimate things, but who abandons himself with confidence in God to provide all that is asked of him and who thus surpasses his own possibilities. And that which God demands of us always goes beyond our natural human possibilities!

3. The Fear of Suffering

The other great obstacle to abandoning oneself to Divine Providence is the presence of suffering, in our own lives as in the world around us. Even for those who abandon themselves to Him, God permits suffering; He leaves them wanting of certain things, in a manner sometimes painful. Think of the poverty in which the family of young Bernadette of Lourdes lived. Isn't this a contradiction of the words of the Gospel? No, because the Lord can leave us wanting relative to certain things (sometimes judged indispensable in the eyes of the world), but He never leaves us deprived of what is essential: His presence, His peace and all that is necessary for the complete fulfillment of our lives, according to His plans for us. If He permits suffering, then it is our strength to believe, as Thérèse of Lisieux says, that "God does not permit unnecessary suffering."

In the domain of our personal lives, as in that of the history of the world, we must be convinced, if we want to go to the limits of our Christian faith, that God is sufficiently good and powerful to use whatever evil there may be, as well as any suffering however absurd and unnecessary it may appear to be, in our favor. We cannot have any mathematical or philosophical certitude of this; it can only be an act of faith. But it is precisely to this act of faith that we are invited by the proclamation of the resurrection of Jesus, understood and received as the definitive victory of God over evil.

Evil is a mystery, a scandal and it will always be so. It is necessary to do what one can to eliminate it, to relieve suffering, but it always remains present in our personal lives, as well as in the world. Its place in the economy of redemption reveals the wisdom of God, which is not the wisdom of man; it always retains something incomprehensible. ...*for My thoughts are not your thoughts, nor are your ways My ways, says the Lord. As high as the heavens are above the earth, so high are My ways above your ways and My thoughts above your thoughts* (Isaiah 55:8-9).

At certain moments in life, a Christian is necessarily invited to believe in the contradiction of appearances and to *hope against all hope* (Romans 4:18). There are inevitably circumstances where we cannot understand the "why" of God's activity because it is no longer the wisdom of man, a wisdom within our capacity to understand and explain by human intelligence. Rather it is divine Wisdom, mysterious and incomprehensible, that thus intervenes.

And *happily* we cannot always understand! Otherwise, how would it be possible to allow the Wisdom of God to freely work according to His designs? Where would there be room for confidence? It is true that for many things we would not act as God would act! We would not have chosen the folly of the cross as a means of redemption! But fortunately it is the Wisdom of God and not ours that rules all things, because it is infinitely more powerful and more loving and, above all, more merciful than ours.

While the Wisdom of God is incomprehensible in its ways, in the sometimes baffling manner in which it acts in us, then let us say that the Wisdom of God will also be incomprehensible in those things that it prepares for those who put their hope in it. For that which it prepares surpasses infinitely in glory and beauty that which we can imagine or conceive: *What eye has not seen nor ear heard, what the human heart has not conceived, what God has prepared for those who love Him, this God has revealed to us through His Spirit* (1 Corinthians 2:9).

The wisdom of man can only produce works on a human level. Only the Wisdom of God can realize things divine, and it is to divine heights that it destines us.

This is consequently what must be our strength when faced with the question of evil: not a philosophical response, but the confidence of a child in God, in His Love and in His Wisdom. The certitude that *Now we know that God works in every way for the good of those who love Him and are called in accordance with His plan* (Romans 8:28) and *the sufferings of the present time simply don't compare with the glory to come that will be revealed to us* (Romans 8:18).

4. To Grow in Confidence: A Child's Prayer

And how does one grow in this total confidence in God; how can we maintain and nourish it in ourselves? Certainly not only by intellectual speculation and theological considerations. They will never withstand the moments of trial. But by a **contemplative gaze on Jesus.**

To contemplate Jesus Who gives His life for us, nourishes us with "too great a love" that He expresses on the cross; that is what really inspires confidence. Would not the supreme proof of love — *Greater love than this no man has than to lay down his life for his friends* (John 15:13) — untiringly contemplated and captured in a gaze of love and faith, fortify our hearts little by little in an unshakable confidence? What can one fear from a God Who manifested His love in so evident a manner? How could He not be **for us**, completely, entirely and absolutely **in our favor**; how could He not do all things for us, this God, friend of humankind, Who *did not spare His only Son for us,* even though we were sinners? And *if God is for us, who could be against us* (Romans 8:32)? If God is for us, what evil could possibly harm us?

Thus, we see the absolute necessity of contemplation for growing in confidence. Finally, too many people are distressed because they are not contemplatives. They do not take the time to nourish their own hearts and return them to peace by gazing with love on Jesus. In order to resist fear and discouragement, it is necessary that through prayer — through a personal experience of God re-encountered, recognized and loved in prayer — we *taste and see how good the Lord is* (Psalm 34). The certitudes that the habit of prayer inculcates in us are considerably stronger than those that flow from reasoning, even at the highest level of theology.

As the assaults of evil, thoughts of discouragement and distrust, are incessant, so, in the same manner and in order to resist them, must our prayers be incessant and untiring. How many times has it happened that I went to make the daily hour of adoration before the Blessed Sacrament in a state of preoccupation or discouragement and, without anything particular having happened, without saying or feeling anything special, I would leave with a quieted heart. The external situation was always the same, there were always problems to solve, but the heart had changed and, from then on, I could confront them peacefully. The Holy Spirit had performed its secret work.

One can never insist enough on the necessity of quiet, meditative prayer — the real source of interior peace. How can one abandon oneself to God and have confidence in Him if one only knows Him from a distance, by hearsay? *I had heard of You by word of mouth, but now my eye has seen You* (Job 42:5). The heart does not awaken to confidence until it awakens to love; we need to feel the gentleness and the tenderness of the Heart of Jesus. This cannot be obtained except by the habit of meditative prayer, by this tender repose in God which is contemplative.

Let us therefore learn to abandon ourselves, to have total confidence in God, in the big things as in the small, with the simplicity of little children. And God will manifest His tenderness, His providence and His fidelity in a manner sometimes overwhelming. If God treats us at certain moments with an apparently great harshness, He also has an unexpected delicateness, of which only a love as tender and pure as His is capable. At the end of his life, Saint John of the Cross, en route to the convent where he would end his days — sick, exhausted, unable to continue — longed for some asparagus, like the asparagus he had eaten in his childhood. Near a rock where he sat to catch his breath, there was a bunch of asparagus, miraculously deposited.

In the midst of our trials, we can experience these delicacies of Love. They are not reserved for the saints. They are for all the poor who believe that God is their Father. They can be for us a powerful encouragement to abandon ourselves to His care, far more efficacious than any reasoning.

And I believe that this is the true response to the mystery of evil and suffering. It is not a philosophical response, but an existential one. In abandoning myself to God, I experience in a concrete fashion that "it really works," that God makes all things work together for my good, even evil, even suffering, even my own sins. How many occasions that I dreaded, when they arrived, in the final analysis proved to be supportable, and finally beneficial, after the first impact of pain. That which I believed to be working against me revealed itself to be to my benefit. Thus, I tell myself: that which God does for me in His infinite Mercy, He must do for others also; in a mysterious and hidden manner, He must do it for the entire world.

5. One Abandons Oneself Completely or Not at All

Relative to the question of abandonment, it is useful to make an observation. In order that abandonment might be authentic and engender peace, it must be total. We must put everything, without exception, into the hands of God, not seeking any longer to manage or "to save" ourselves by our own means: not in the material domain, nor the emotional, nor the spiritual. We cannot divide human existence into various sectors: certain sectors where it would be legitimate to surrender ourselves to God with confidence and others where, on the contrary, we feel we must manage exclusively on our own. And one thing we know well: all reality that we have not surrendered to God, that we choose to manage by ourselves without giving *carte blanche* to God, will continue to make us more or less uneasy. The measure of our interior peace will be that of our abandonment, consequently of our detachment.

Abandonment inevitably requires an element of renunciation and it is this that is most difficult for us. We have a natural tendency to cling to a whole host of things: material goods, affections, desires, projects, etc. and it costs us terribly to let go of our grip, because we have the impression that we will lose ourselves in the process, that we will die. But that is why we must believe with all our hearts the words of Jesus, that law of "who loses gains," which is so explicit in the Gospel: *Whoever would save his life will lose it, while whoever loses his life for My sake will find it* (Matthew 16:25). He who accepts this death of detachment, of renunciation, finds the true life. The one who clings to something, who wishes to protect some domain in his life in order to manage it at his convenience without radically abandoning it into the hands of God, is making a very bad mistake: he devotes himself to unnecessary preoccupations and exposes himself to the gnawing sense of loss. By contrast, he who accepts to put everything into the hands of God, to allow Him to give and take according to His good pleasure, this individual finds an inexpressible peace and interior freedom. "Ah, if one only knew what one gains in renouncing all things!", Saint Thérèse of the Child Jesus tells us. This is the way to happiness, because if we leave God free to act in His way, He is infinitely more capable of rendering us happy than we ourselves are, because He knows us and loves us more than we can ever know or love ourselves. Saint John of the Cross expresses this same truth in other terms: "All things were given to me from the moment when I no longer sought them." If we detach ourselves from everything and put them into the hands of God, God will return them to us a hundredfold, *from this day forward* (1 Maccabees 10:30).

6. God Asks For Everything, But He Doesn't Necessarily Take Everything

With regard to what we have just considered, it is important to know how to unmask a frequent and very clever trick of the devil to trouble and discourage us. Faced with certain goods that we possess (a material good, a friendship, an activity that we enjoy, etc.), the devil, in an effort to prevent us from abandoning ourselves to God, causes us to imagine that if we put everything in God's hands, God will effectively take everything and "ruin" everything in our lives! And this arouses a sense of terror that completely paralyzes us. But we must not fall into this trap. Very frequently, on the contrary, the Lord asks only an attitude of detachment at the level of the heart, a disposition to give Him everything. But He doesn't necessarily "take" everything. He leaves us in peaceful possession of many things when they are not bad in themselves and can serve His designs, knowing how to reassure us with respect to scruples that we might have in enjoying certain goods, certain human joys, scruples that one frequently finds in those who love the Lord and want to do His will. And we must firmly believe that if God requires effective detachment of us, relative to this or that reality, He will have us clearly understand this in good time. He will give us the necessary strength. And this detachment, even though it is painful at the moment, will be followed by a profound peace. The proper attitude then is simply to be disposed to give everything to God, without panic, and to allow Him to do things His way, in total confidence.

7. What to Do When You Are Unable to Abandon Yourself?

We posed this question to Marthe Robin. Her response was: "Abandon yourself anyway!" This is the response of a saint and I cannot permit myself to propose another. She adds her voice to that of Saint Thérèse of the Child Jesus: "Total abandonment; that's my only law!"

Abandonment is not natural; it is a grace to be asked of God. He will give it to us, if we pray with perseverance: *Ask, and it will be given to you* (Matthew 7:7).

Abandonment is a fruit of the Holy Spirit, but the Lord does not refuse this Spirit to those who ask with faith: *If you, then, who are evil, know how to give your children what is good, how much more will the heavenly Father give the Holy Spirit to those who ask Him!* (Luke 11:13).

8. The Lord is My Shepherd, I Shall Not Want

One of the most beautiful expressions in the Bible of confident abandonment into the hands of God is Psalm 23:

The LORD is my shepherd, I shall not want.
In verdant pastures He gives me repose.
Beside restful waters He leads me;
He refreshes my soul.
He guides me in right paths,
For His name's sake.
Even though I walk through a dark valley,
I fear no evil; for You are at my side
With Your rod and Your staff
that give me courage.
You spread a table before me
In the sight of my foes;
You anoint my head with oil;
My cup overflows.
Only goodness and kindness follow me,
All the days of my life
And I shall dwell in the house of the LORD
for years to come!

We would like to come back for a few moments to this affirmation of the Bible, which is ultimately surprising, that God leaves us wanting for nothing. This will serve to unmask a temptation, sometimes subtle, which is very common in the

Christian life, one into which many fall and which greatly impedes spiritual progress.

It concerns precisely the temptation to believe that, in the situation which is ours (personal, family, etc.), we lack something essential and that because of this, our progress, and the possibility of blossoming spiritually, is denied us.

For example, I lack good health, therefore I am unable to pray as I believe it is indispensable to do. Or my immediate family prevents me from organizing my spiritual activities as I wish. Or, again, I don't have the qualities, the strength, the virtue, the gifts that I believe necessary in order to accomplish something beautiful for God, according to the plan of a Christian life. I am not satisfied with my life, with my person, with my circumstances and I live constantly with the feeling that as long as things are such, it will be impossible for me to live truly and intensely. I feel underprivileged compared to others and I carry in me the constant nostalgia of another life, more privileged, where, finally, I could do things that are worthwhile.

I have the feeling, according to Rimbaud's expression, that "the real life is elsewhere," elsewhere than in the life that is mine. And that the latter is not a real life, that it doesn't offer me the conditions for real spiritual growth because of certain sufferances or limitations. I am concentrated on the negatives of my situation, on that which I lack in order to be happy. This renders me unhappy,

envious and discouraged and I am unable to go forward. The real life is elsewhere, I tell myself, and I
simply forget to live. Oftentimes it would take so
little for everything to be different and for me to
progress with giant steps: a different outlook, a view
of my situation which is one of confidence and hope
(based on the certitude that I will lack nothing).
And then doors would open to me of unhoped-for
possibilities for spiritual growth.

We often live with this illusion. With the
impression that all would go better, we would like
the things around us to change, that the circumstances would change. But this is often an error. It
is not the exterior circumstances that must change;
it is above all our hearts that must change. They
must be purified of their withdrawal into themselves, of their sadness, of their lack of hope: *Happy
are the pure in heart; they shall see God* (Matthew 5:8).
Happy are those whose hearts are purified by faith
and hope, who bring to their lives a view animated
by the certitude that, beyond appearances to the
contrary, God is present, providing for their essential needs and that they lack nothing. If they have
that faith, they will indeed see God: they will experience that presence of God which will accom-
pany them and guide them. They will see that many
of the circumstances that they thought negative and
damaging to their spiritual life are, in fact, in God's
pedagogy, powerful means for helping them to
progress and grow. Saint John of the Cross says that

"it is very often the case that just when the soul believes itself lost that it gains and profits most." This is very true.

Our minds are sometimes so clouded over by that which is not going well, by that which (according to our own particular criteria!) should be different in our situations, that we forget the positive. Moreover, we are unable to profit from any aspect of our situations, even the aspects that only appear to be negative, in order for us to draw closer to God, to grow in faith, love and humility. That which we lack is, above all, the conviction that "the love of God turns to profit all that he finds in me, the good as well as the bad" (Saint Thérèse of the Child Jesus, inspired by John of the Cross). However many imperfections we may have, rather than lament them and try to rid ourselves of them at any price, they could be splendid opportunities to make progress — in humility as well as in confidence in God and His mercy — and thus in saintliness.

The fundamental problem is that we employ too much of our own criteria as to what is and what is not good and we don't have enough confidence in the Wisdom and Power of God. We don't believe that He is capable of utilizing everything for our good and that never, under any circumstance, would He leave us lacking in the essentials — that is to say, lacking anything that would permit us to love more. Because, to grow or to enrich one's spiritual life is to learn to love. Many of the circumstances that I consider damaging could, in fact, be for me, if I had more faith, precious opportunities to love more: to be more patient, more humble, more gentle, more merciful and to abandon myself more into the hands of God.

Let us then be convinced of this and it will be for us a source of immense strength: God may allow me to occasionally lack money, health, abilities and virtues, but He will never leave me in want of Himself, of His assistance and His mercy or of anything that would allow me to grow unceasingly ever closer to Him, to love Him more intensely, to better love my neighbor and to achieve holiness.

9. Attitude When Confronted With the Suffering of Those Close to Us

A situation in which we frequently risk losing our peace of soul is that in which someone close to us finds himself in difficulty. We sometimes feel more troubled and preoccupied by the suffering of a friend or a child than by our own suffering. In itself, this may be fine and good, but it must never become an occasion for despair. How much excessive anxiety sometimes reigns in families when a member is tested in matters of health, unemployment, depression, etc. How many parents torment themselves over a problem concerning one of their children, for example.

The Lord, however, invites us not to lose our interior peace in these instances either, for all the reasons already enumerated in the preceding pages. Our distress is legitimate, but we must remain peaceful. The Lord does not know how to abandon us: *Can a mother forget her infant, or be without tenderness for the child of her womb? Yet even should she forget, I will never forget you* (Isaiah 49:15).

There is one point, however, on which we wish to insist, and it is this: as we shall see by the following, it is equally important to clearly know how to distinguish between true and false humility, between real, peaceful and confident repentance and false, disturbing remorse which paralyzes, as it is to know how to distinguish between that which we might call true and false compassion.

It is certain that the more we advance in the Christian life, the more our compassion grows. While we are naturally hard and indifferent, the spectacle of misery in the world and the suffering of their brothers draws tears from the saints whose intimacy with Jesus has "melted" their hearts, according to the expression of the Curé of Ars. Saint Dominic spent his nights in prayer and in tears pleading with the Lord: "Merciful God, what will become of sinners?" And one could rightly doubt the value of the spiritual life of a person who does not manifest a growing compassion.

However, the compassion of the saints, if it is profound and quick to marry all misery and come to its relief is nevertheless always tender, peaceful and confident. It is the fruit of the Spirit.

On the contrary, our compassion for ourselves is often disturbed and anxious. We have a way of implicating ourselves in the suffering of others that is not always correct, that sometimes proceeds more from a love of self than from a true love of others. And we believe that to preoccupy ourselves excessively with another in difficulty is justified, that it is a sign of the love that we feel for the other person. But this is false. There is often in this attitude a great, hidden love of ourselves. We cannot bear the suffering of others because we are afraid of suffering ourselves. The reason is that we, too, lack confidence in God.

It is normal to be profoundly touched by the suffering of another who is dear to us, but if, because of this, we torment ourselves to the point of losing our peace, this signifies that our love for the other person is still not fully spiritual, is still not in harmony with God. It is a love that is still too human and, without doubt, egotistical, whose foundation is not sufficiently based on an unshakable confidence in God.

In order for it to be a true Christian virtue, compassion for others must proceed from love (which consists in desiring the good of others, in the light of God and in accord with His designs) and not from fear (fear of suffering, fear of losing something). But, in fact, all too often our attitude toward those around us who are suffering is more conditioned by fear than love.

One thing is certain: God loves our dear ones infinitely more than we do, and infinitely better. He wants us to believe in this love, and also to know how to entrust those who are dear to us into His hands. And this will often be a much more efficacious way of helping them.

Our brothers and sisters who suffer need peaceful, confident and joyful people around them and will be helped much more effectively by them than by those who are preoccupied and anxious. Our false compassion often only adds to their sadness and distress. It is not a source of peace and hope for those who suffer.

I would like to give a concrete example that I encountered very recently. It concerns a young woman who suffers greatly from a form of depression, with fears and anxieties that often prevent her from going alone to the city. I spoke with her mother who was discouraged and in tears, and who begged me to pray for her daughter's healing. I respect infinitely the understandable pain of this mother. And we, of course, prayed for her daughter. But, what struck me is that when, a little later, I had occasion to speak with this young woman herself, I came to realize that she bore her suffering in peace. She said to me: "I am incapable of praying, and the only thing that I do not cease to say to Jesus are the words of the Twenty-third

Psalm: *The Lord is my shepherd, I shall not want."* She also told me that she saw positive fruits from her illness, particularly in her father, who, in the past had been very harsh with her, but had now changed his demeanor.

I have often seen cases of this type: a person is undergoing a trial, but she manages this trial better than those around her, who are concerned and troubled. There can be at times a way of multiplying prayers for healing, even of seeing a cure, of pursuing all the means possible and imaginable for obtaining the deliverance of this person, without being aware that the hand of God is clearly behind it all. I do not say that one should not support those who are suffering by persevering prayers and petitions for their healing, nor that we should not do what is humanly and spiritually possible to obtain it. It is our duty to do these things, to be sure. But we should do so in a spirit of peace and confident abandonment into the hands of God.

10. In All People Who Suffer There is Jesus

The most decisive motive to aid us in peacefully confronting the drama of suffering is this: we must take very seriously the mystery of the Incarnation and that of the Cross. Jesus took our flesh, He really took upon Himself our sufferings. And in all people who suffer there is Jesus who suffers.

In the Gospel according to Saint Matthew, chapter 25, in the narrative on the Last Judgment, Jesus says to those who took care of the sick or visited prisoners: *Insofar as you did it for one of these least of My brothers, you did it for Me.* These words of the Lord teach us that "on the eve of our life we will be judged by how much we loved" (Saint John of the Cross) and in particular how much we loved our brothers in need. It is an exhortation to compassion. But, these words of Jesus, do they not invite us also to recognize His traits, His presence in all those who suffer? They call us to apply ourselves with all our strength to relieve this suffering, but also to view it with hope. In all suffering there is a germ of life and of the resurrection, because Jesus is there in person.

If, in confronting a person who is suffering, we have this conviction that it is Jesus Who is suffering in this person, Who in this person completes that which is lacking in His Passion, to speak like Saint Paul, how can one despair in the face of this suffering? Is His passion not redemptive? Do not *grieve as other people do who have no hope* (1 Thessalonians 4:13).

11. The Faults and Shortcomings of Others

I stated that disquietude, in the face of some evil that threatens or overcomes our own person or those who are dear to us, is the most frequent reason why we lose our interior peace.

And the response: confident abandonment into the hands of God, Who delivers us from all evil, or Who, if He allows it, gives us the strength to endure it and makes it turn to our advantage.

This response will remain valid for all the other causes for losing our peace, with which we will now interest ourselves and which are specific cases. Nevertheless, it is good to speak of it because though abandonment may be the sole rule, the practice of abandonment takes diverse forms according to what is at the origin of our troubles and our anxieties.

It often happens that we lose our peace not because suffering affects us or threatens to affect us personally, but rather because of the behavior of an individual person or group of persons who hurt us or preoccupy us. It is thus something that is not directly ours — but which nonetheless concerns us — that is in question: for example, the good of our community, of the Church or the salvation of a particular person.

A woman is perhaps distressed because she does not see a much desired conversion of her husband being realized. A superior of a community may lose his sense of peace, because one of his brothers or sisters does the contrary of that which he expects. Or, more simply, in everyday life, one becomes irritated, because one close to him behaves in a way that he imagines he should not behave. How many nervous tensions are due to this type of situation!

The response is the same as previously indicated: confidence and abandonment. I must do what occurs to me relative to aiding others to improve themselves, peacefully and tenderly, and put everything else in the hands of the Lord, Who knows how to draw benefit from all things.

But, relative to this, we would like to express a general principle that is very important in our daily spiritual life and which is the point at which we usually stumble in the cases cited above. In addition, its area of application is much larger than the question of patience when confronted with the faults of others.

Here is the principle: Not only must we be careful to want and desire good things for their own sake, but also to want and desire them in a way that is good. To be attentive not only to **that** which we want, but also to the **way** in which we want them. In effect, we very frequently sin in this fashion: We want something which is good, and even very good, but we want it in a way that is bad. In order to understand, let us take one of the examples mentioned above. It is normal that the superior of a community should watch over the sanctity of those in his care. It's an excellent thing and conforms to the will of God. But if this superior gets angry, irritated or loses his peace over the imperfections or the lack of fervor of his brothers, it is certainly not the Holy Spirit that is animating him. And we often have this tendency. Because the thing that we want is good, even seen as desired by God, we feel justified in wanting it with that much more impatience and displeasure if it is not realized. The more a thing seems good to us, the more we are agitated and preoccupied to realize it!

We should, therefore, as I have said, not only verify that the things we want are good in themselves, but also that the manner in which we want them, the disposition of heart in which we want them, are good. That is to say that our wanting must always be caring, peaceful, patient, detached and abandoned to God. It should not be an impatient wanting, hurried, restless, irritated, etc. In the spiritual life it is often there that our attitude is defective. We are no longer among those who want bad things that are contrary to God. Instead, from now on we want only those things that are good, in conformity with the will of God. But, we want them in a manner that is still not "God's way," that is to say the way of the Holy Spirit, which is caring, peaceful and patient. We want them in a human way, tense, hurried and discouraged if we do not immediately achieve the desired goal.

All of the saints insist on telling us that we must moderate our desires, even the best of them. Because, if we desire in the human way that we have described, that will trouble the soul, make it uneasy, destroy its peace and thereby disturb God's actions in it and in others.

This applies to all things, even to our own sanctification. How many times do we lose our peace because we find that our sanctification is not progressing rapidly enough, that we still have too many faults? But this does nothing but delay things! Saint Francis de Sales goes so far as to say that "nothing retards progress in a virtue so much as wanting to acquire it with too much haste!" But we will come back to this point in a later chapter.

To conclude, let us keep this in mind: As far as all our desires and our wishes are concerned, the sign that we are in accordance with truth, that our desire is in accord with the Holy Spirit, is not only that the thing desired is good, it is also that we are at peace. A desire that causes us to lose peace, even if the thing desired is excellent in itself, is not of God. It is necessary to want and desire, but in a free and detached way, in abandoning to God the realization of these desires, as He desires and when He wishes. To educate our own heart in this sense is of great importance for our spiritual progress. It is God Who converts us and causes us to grow, not our nervousness, our impetuosity and our impatience.

12. Patience Towards Others

Let us apply this then to a desire that we have that others around us would behave better: that this desire would be peaceful and without distress. Let us know how to remain calm even when others around us act in a manner that seems to us erroneous and unjust. We should clearly do what depends on us to help them, even to see that they are reproved or corrected, in line with the potential responsibilities that we have to assume with regard to them, but everything should be done in gentleness and peace. When we are powerless, let us be quiet and let God act.

How many people lose their peace because they want, at any price, to change those around them! How many married people become agitated and irritated because they would like their spouses not to have this or that fault! The Lord asks us, on the contrary, to bear with patience the faults of others.

We must reason as follows: if the Lord has still not transformed this person, has not relieved him of such and such an imperfection, it is because He puts up with him as he is! He waits, with patience, the opportune moment. Then I must do likewise. I must pray and be patient. Why be more demanding and impatient than God? I think sometimes that my haste is motivated by love. But, God loves infinitely more than I do; however He is less hurried! *Therefore be patient, brothers, until the coming of the Lord. Think of the farmer: how he waits for the precious yield of the earth, patiently waiting until it receives the early and late rains!* (James 5:7).

This patience is all the more important in that it brings about in us a purification that is absolutely indispensable. We believe that we wish the good of others, or our own good, but this wish is frequently mixed with a great deal of hidden search for oneself, our own will, our attachment to personal beliefs, narrow and limited, to which we cling so much and that we wish to impose on others and sometimes even on God. We must at all costs be free of this narrowness of heart and judgment, in order that it is the good, not such as we imagine it or conceive it, that is realized, but that which corresponds to the designs of God, so much more vast and appealing.

13. Patience Vis-à-vis Our Own Faults and Imperfections

When one has gone a certain distance in spiritual life, when one truly desires to love the Lord with all his heart, when one has learned to have confidence in God and to abandon himself into His hands in the midst of difficulties, there remains for him, however, a circumstance in which he often risks losing his peace and tranquility of soul and which the devil frequently exploits to discourage and trouble him.

It concerns the vision of his misery, the experience of his own faults, the failures he continues to experience in such and such an area, despite his strong desire to correct himself.

But here also it is important to be aware that the sadness, the discouragement and the anguish of soul that we feel after committing a fault are not good and we must, on the contrary, do everything we can to remain at peace.

In the daily experience of our miseries and faults, this is the fundamental principle that must guide us. It is not so much a question of our making superhuman efforts to completely eliminate our imperfections and our sins (that which is, in any case, beyond our reach!), as it is a question of knowing how, as quickly as possible, to recapture our peace when we have fallen into sin or have been troubled by the experience of our imperfections, and to avoid sadness and discouragement.

This is not laxity, nor resignation to mediocrity, but, on the contrary, a way in which to sanctify ourselves more rapidly. There are a number of reasons for this.

The first reason is the fundamental principle that we have already mentioned many times: God acts in the peace of one's soul. It is not by our own efforts that we succeed in liberating ourselves from sin; it is only the grace of God which attains this end. Rather than troubling ourselves, it is more efficacious to regain our peace and let God act.

The second reason is that this is more pleasing to God. What is more pleasing to God? Is it when, after experiencing a failure, we are discouraged and tormented, or when we react by saying: "Lord, I ask Your pardon, I have sinned again. This, alas, is what I am capable of doing on my own! But I abandon myself with confidence to Your mercy and Your pardon, I thank You for not allowing me to sin even more grievously. I abandon myself to You with confidence because I know that one day You will heal me completely and, in the meantime, I ask You that the experience of my misery would cause me to be more humble, more considerate of others, more conscious that I can do nothing by myself, but that I must rely solely on Your love and Your mercy." The response is clear.

The third reason is that the trouble, the sadness and the discouragement that we feel regarding our failures and our faults are rarely pure; they are not very often the simple pain of having offended God. They are in good part mixed with pride. We are not sad and discouraged so much because God was offended, but because the ideal image that we have of ourselves has been brutally shaken. Our pain is very often that of wounded pride! This excessive pain is actually a sign that we have put our trust in ourselves — in our own strength and not in God. Listen to Dom Lorenzo Scupoli whom we have already cited:

A presumptuous man believes with certainty that he has acquired a distrust of himself and confidence in God (which are the foundations of the spiritual life and therefore that which one must make an effort to acquire), but this is an error that we never recognize better than when we have just experienced a failure. Because then, if one is troubled by it, if one feels afflicted by it, if it causes one to lose all hope of making new progress in virtue, this is a sign that one has placed all his confidence, not in God, but in himself, and the greater the sadness and despair, the more one must judge himself guilty.

Because he who mistrusts himself greatly and who puts great confidence in God, if he commits some fault, is hardly surprised, he is neither disturbed nor chagrined because he sees clearly that this is the result of his weakness and the little care he took to establish his confidence in God. His failure, on the contrary, teaches him to distrust even more his own strength and to put even greater trust in the help of Him who alone has power: he detests above all his sin; he condemns the passion or vicious habit which was the cause;

he conceives a sharp pain for having offended his God, but his pain is always subdued and does not prevent him from returning to his primary occupations, to bear with his familiar trials and to battle until death with his cruel enemies....

It is, again, a very common illusion to attribute to a feeling of virtue this fear and trouble that one experiences after a sin: because, though the uneasiness that follows the sin is always accompanied by some pain, still it does not proceed only from a source of pride or from a secret presumption, caused by too great a confidence in one's own strength. Thus, then, whoever believes himself affirmed in virtue, is contemptuous toward temptations and comes to understand, by the sad experience of his failures, that he is fragile and a sinner like others, is surprised, as if by something that never should have happened; and, deprived of the feeble support on which he was counting, he allows himself to succumb to chagrin and despair.

This misfortune never happens to those who are humble, who do not presume on themselves and who rely only on God: when they have failed, they are neither surprised nor chagrined because the light of truth which illuminates them makes them see that it is a natural result of their weakness and their inconstancy. (*The Spiritual Combat & A Treatise on Peace of Soul,* William Lester and Robert Mohan, trs., TAN Books & Publishers, 1993, chapters 4 and 5)

14. God Can Draw Good Even From Our Faults

The fourth reason for which this sadness and discouragement are not good is that we must not view our own faults too tragically because God is able to draw good from them. Little Thérèse of the Child Jesus loved greatly this phrase of Saint John of the Cross: "Love is able to profit from everything, the good as well as the bad that It finds in me, and to transform it into Itself."

Our confidence in God must go at least that far: to believe that He is good enough and powerful enough to draw good from everything, including our faults and our infidelities.

When he cites the phrase of Saint Paul, *Everything works together for the good of those who love God,* Saint Augustine adds: *Etiam peccata* — "even sins"!

Of course, we must struggle energetically against sin and correct our imperfections. God vomits the tepid, and nothing cools love quite like resigning oneself to mediocrity (this resignation is, by the way, a lack of confidence in God and His ability to sanctify us!). When we have been the cause of some evil, we must also try to rectify it to the extent that this is possible. But we must not distress ourselves excessively regarding our faults because God, once we return to Him with a contrite heart, is able to cause good to spring forth, if only to make us to grow in humility and to teach us to have a little less confidence in our own strength and a little more in Him alone.

So great is the mercy of the Lord that He uses our faults to our advantage! Ruysbroek, a Flemish mystic of the Middle Ages, has these words: "The Lord, in His clemency, wanted to turn our sins against themselves and in our favor; He found a way to render them useful, to convert them in our hands into instruments of salvation. This should in no way diminish our fear of sinning, nor our pain at having sinned. Rather, our sins have become for us a source of humility."

Let us add also that they can just as well become a source of tenderness and mercy toward others. I, who fall so easily, how can I permit myself to judge my brother? How can I not be merciful toward him, as the Lord has been toward me?

Accordingly, after committing a fault of whatever kind, rather than withdrawing into ourselves indefinitely in discouragement and dwelling on the memory, we must immediately return to God with confidence and even thank Him for the good that His mercy will be able to draw out of this fault!

We must know that one of the weapons that the devil uses most commonly to prevent souls from advancing toward God is precisely to try to make them lose their peace and discourage them by the sight of their faults.

It is necessary that we know how to distinguish true repentance and a true desire to correct our faults, which is always gentle, peaceful, trustful, from a false repentance, from that remorse that troubles, discourages and paralyzes. Not all of the reproaches that come to our conscience are inspired by the Holy Spirit! Some of them come from our pride or the devil and we must learn to discern them. Peace is an essential criterion in the discernment of spirits. The feelings that come from the Spirit of God can be very powerful and profound, nonetheless, they are always peaceful. Let us listen again to Scupoli:

> To preserve our hearts in perfect tranquility, it is still necessary to ignore some interior feelings of remorse which seem to come from God, because they are reproaches that our conscience makes to us regarding true faults, but which come, in effect, from the evil spirit as can be judged by what ensues. If the twinges of conscience serve to make us more humble, if they render us more fervent in the practice of good works, if they do not diminish the trust that one must have in divine

mercy, we must accept them with thanksgiving, as favors from heaven. But if they trouble us, if they dishearten us, if they render us lazy, timid, slow to perform our duties, we must believe that these are the suggestions of the enemy and **do things in a normal way, not deigning to listen to them**. (*The Spiritual Combat,* chapter 25)

Let us understand this: For the person of goodwill, that which is serious in sin is not so much the fault in itself as the despondency into which it places him. He who falls but immediately gets up has not lost much. He has rather gained in humility and in the experience of mercy. He who remains sad and defeated loses much more. The sign of spiritual progress is not so much never falling as it is being able to lift oneself up quickly after one falls.

15. What Should We Do When We Have Sinned?

From all that we have just said, there flows a rule of conduct that is very important to keep in mind when we should happen to commit a fault. We certainly must feel sorry for having sinned, ask God for pardon, humbly beg Him to accord us the grace not to offend Him again in this way, and resolve to go to confession at an opportune moment.

Without making ourselves sad or discouraged, we should recover our peace as quickly as possible thanks to graces from on high, and resume our normal spiritual life as if nothing had happened. The more quickly we recover our peace, the better it will be! We make much more progress in this way than by becoming irritated with ourselves!

A very important, concrete example is the following: when we commit some fault or other, under the assault of a trial that seizes us, we are often tempted to grow slack in our prayer life, to not spend, for example, our usual time in silent meditation. And we manage to find good justification for this: "How can I who have just fallen into sin, who have offended the Lord, how can I present myself before Him in this state?" And we need sometimes several days before we can resume our normal habits of prayer. But this is a grave error; this is nothing but false humility inspired by the devil. We must above all not change our habits of prayer. Quite the contrary. Where will we find healing for our faults if not close to Jesus? Our sins are a very poor pretext for distancing ourselves from Him, because the more we sin, the more we have a right precisely to approach Him who says: *The healthy are not in need of a doctor — the sick are.... Indeed I came not to call the righteous, but sinners* (Matthew 9:12-13).

If we wait until we are saints to have a regular life of prayer, we could wait a long time. On the contrary, it is in accepting to appear before the Lord in our state of sin that we will receive healing and will be transformed, little by little, into saints.

There is an important illusion that must be exposed: we would like to present ourselves before the Lord only when we are presentable, well-groomed and content with ourselves! But there is a lot of presumptuousness in that attitude! In effect, we would like to bypass the need for mercy. But what is the nature of this pseudo-sanctity to which we sometimes aspire unconsciously and which would result in our thinking that we no longer have need of God? True sanctity is, on the contrary, to increasingly recognize how much we absolutely depend upon His mercy!

To conclude, let us cite a last passage from *The Spiritual Combat* that recaptures everything we have said and indicates to us the path we should take when we have committed some kind of fault. It is entitled, "What one must do when one receives a wound in spiritual battle!"

> When you feel wounded, that is to say, when you feel that you have committed some fault, whether it be from pure weakness or with reflection and malice, do not distress yourself too much over that; do not allow yourself to become chagrined and irritated; but address yourself immediately to God and tell Him, with humble confidence: "It is now, oh, my God, that I can see what I am. For

what can one expect from a weak and blind creature like me but wrongdoing and failure?" Stop yourself there and imagine a sharp pain because of your fault.

Then, without becoming troubled, turn all of your anger against the passions that dominate you, principally against those that were the cause of your sin.

Lord, you will say, I could have committed a much worse crime if by your infinite goodness you had not saved me.

Afterwards, render a thousand thanks to the Father of Mercies; love Him more than ever, seeing that, far from resenting the hurt that you just caused Him, He still extends His hand to you, for fear that you will fall again into a similar mess.

Finally, full of confidence, tell Him: "Show me, oh, my God, that which you are; help a humiliated sinner to feel your divine mercy; forgive me all my offenses; do not permit me to separate or distance myself from you, however little; fortify me with your grace, so that I may never offend you again."

After that, don't try to determine whether God has pardoned you or not. That would be to upset yourself uselessly. It is a waste of time. It stems from pride and the illusions of the devil who, by disquieting your spirit, seeks to harm and torment you.

Rather, abandon yourself to His divine mercy and continue your exercises with your usual tranquility as if you had hardly committed any fault. Even should you have offended God several times in a single day, never lose confidence in Him. Practice what I tell you, the second, the third and the last time as the first.... This way of combating the devil is the one that he fears the most because he knows that it pleases God very much and it always throws him into a great confusion, seeing himself overcome by the very person he was able to conquer so easily in other encounters.

So, if a fault that you may unfortunately have committed causes you to be troubled and discouraged, the first thing that you should do is to try to recover your peace of soul and your confidence in God...

To finish this point, we would like to add a remark: It is true that it is dangerous to do wrong and we must do everything we can to avoid doing wrong. But let us recognize that, given the way we are made, it would be dangerous for us to do only good!

In effect, marked by original sin, we have a deeply rooted tendency toward pride that makes it difficult for us, and even impossible, to do good without appropriating a little of it for ourselves, without attributing it, at least in part, to our abilities, our merits or our sanctity! If the Lord did not permit us, from time to time, to do wrong, to acquire some imperfection, we would be in great danger! We would quickly fall into presumptuousness and contempt of others. We would forget that everything comes freely from God.

And nothing precludes true love more than this pride. In order to protect us from this great evil, the Lord sometimes allows a lesser evil which consists in committing some kind of fault, and we should thank Him for that, because without this safety net we would be in great danger of being lost!

16. Unrest When We Have Decisions to Make

The last reason that we are going to examine and which frequently causes us to lose our sense of peace is lack of certitude, the troubling of conscience that is experienced when it is necessary to make a decision and we are not able to see clearly. We are afraid to make a mistake that may have disturbing consequences, we are afraid that it may not be the will of the Lord.

Situations of this type can be very painful and certain dilemmas truly agonizing. The general stance of abandonment and confidence of which we have spoken, this approach of putting everything into the hands of God which enables us to avoid "dramatizing" anything (even the consequences that our errors might engender!) will be particularly precious in these situations of incertitude.

We would like, however, to make a few useful remarks for conserving our interior peace when making decisions.

The first thing to say (and this is in complete harmony with what we have said up to this point) is that, faced with an important decision, one of the errors to avoid is that of being excessively hurried or precipitous. A certain deliberation is often necessary in order to properly consider things and to allow our hearts to orient themselves peaceably and gently toward a good solution. Saint Vincent de Paul made decisions that were presented to him after mature reflection (and above all prayer!), in such a way that some people who were close to him found him too slow to decide. But, one judges a tree by its fruit!

Before making a decision, it is necessary to do what is appropriate to see the situation clearly and not to decide precipitously or arbitrarily. We need to analyze the situation with its different aspects and to consider our motivations in order to decide with a pure heart and not in an effort to serve our personal interests. We need to pray for the light of the Holy Spirit and the grace to act in conformity with the will of God and, if necessary, to ask the advice of people who can enlighten us relative to this decision.

In this regard, we must know that everyone

will encounter, above all in the spiritual life, certain situations where one would not have sufficient light, would be incapable of making a necessary discernment or of making a determination in peace, without recourse to a spiritual advisor. The Lord does not want us to be self-sufficient and, as part of His pedagogy, He permits that sometime we find ourselves in the impossibility of finding enlightenment and peace by ourselves; we cannot receive them except through the intermediary of another person to whom we can open up. There is, in this opening up of the heart relative to questions that we ask ourselves or dilemmas that we try to solve, a disposition of humility and trust which greatly pleases the Lord and frequently renders harmless the traps that the enemy sets there to deceive or trouble us. Regarding this interior peace, which is so precious and of which we have spoken so much, we know that at certain moments in our lives we cannot find it by ourselves without the help of someone to whom we can open our souls. Saint Alphonsus Liguori was an unparalleled director of souls, but with regard to that which concerned his own spiritual life, he was very often incapable of orienting himself without the aid of someone to whom he opened himself and toward whom he was obedient.

Having said that, it is important to know one thing. Whatever the precautions (prayer, reflection, advice) that one uses to obtain enlightenment before making a decision and in order to be sure of doing God's will (it's a duty to take these precautions, because we do not have the right, above all in domains of importance, to decide lightly), one will not always receive this light in a clear and unambiguous manner. Confronted with a specific situation, we ask ourselves (and we must always do this!): "What must I do? What is the Lord's will?" We will not always have a response!

When we make this effort at discernment and search for God's will, often the Lord speaks to us in diverse ways and makes us understand in a clear way how we must act. Then we can make our decision in peace.

But, it may happen that the Lord does not respond to us. And this is completely normal. Sometimes, He simply leaves us free and sometimes, for reasons of His own, He does not manifest Himself. It is good to know this, because it often happens that people, for fear of making a mistake, of not doing the will of God, seek at any price to have an answer. They increase their reflections, their prayers, they open the Bible ten times looking for a text in order to obtain the desired enlightenment. And all this is troubling and disquieting more than anything else. We do not see things more clearly for all that; we have a text, but we don't know how to interpret it.

When the Lord leaves us thus in incertitude, we must quietly accept it. Rather than wanting to "force things" and torment ourselves unnecessarily because we do not have an evident response, we must follow the principle that Saint Faustina offers us:

> When one does not know what is best, one must reflect, consider and take counsel, because one does not have the right to act in incertitude of conscience. In incertitude (if the incertitude remains) one must tell oneself: whatever I do, it will be good, provided that I have the intention to do good. That which we consider good, God accepts and considers as good. Don't be chagrined if, after a certain time, you see that these things are not good. God looks at the intention with which we begin and He grants the reward according to this intention. It is a principle that we must follow. (*Divine Mercy in My Soul: The Diary of the Servant of God, Sister Faustina Kowalska,* Marian Press, 1988, No. 799)

Often we torment ourselves excessively regarding our decisions. As there is a false humility, a false compassion, we can also say that, concerning our decisions, there is sometimes that which one could call a "false obedience" to God. We would like always to be absolutely certain of doing God's will in all of our choices and never to be mistaken. But, there is, in this attitude, something that is not exactly right for a variety of reasons.

For one thing, this desire to know what God wants sometimes hides a difficulty in enduring a situation of incertitude. We want to be released from having to decide by ourselves. But, frequently, the will of the Lord is that we do decide for ourselves, even if we are not absolutely sure that this decision would be the best. In effect, in this capacity to decide in incertitude, in doing that which seems to us best without spending hours equivocating, there is an attitude of confidence and abandonment: "Lord, I have thought about it and prayed to know Your will. I do not see it clearly, but I am not going to trouble myself any further. I am not going to spend hours racking my brain. I am deciding such and such a thing because, all things carefully considered, it seems to me the best thing to do. And I leave everything in Your hands. I know well that, even if I am mistaken, You will not be displeased with me, for I have acted with good intentions. And if I have made a mistake, I know that You are able to draw good from this error. It will be for me a source of humility and I will learn something from it!" And I remain at peace.

For another thing, we would love to be infallible, to never be wrong, but there is a lot of pride in this desire and there is also the fear of being judged by others. The one, on the contrary, who accepts peacefully the idea of being wrong from time to time and accepts that others know it manifests true humility and a true love of God.

On the other hand, let us not have a false idea of what God requires of us. God is our Father, good and compassionate, Who knows the shortcomings of His children, the limitations of our judgment. He asks of us goodwill, the right intentions, but in no way does He demand that we would be infallible and that all of our decisions would be perfect! And additionally, if all our decisions were perfect, this would, without doubt, do us more harm than good! We would quickly take ourselves for supermen.

To conclude, the Lord loves him more who knows how to decide for himself without equivocating, even when he is uncertain, and who abandons himself with confidence to God as to the consequences, rather than the one who torments his spirit unceasingly in an effort to know what God expects of him and who never decides. Because, there is, in the first attitude, more abandonment, confidence and therefore love, than in the second. God loves those who make their way with freedom of spirit and who don't "split hairs" too much over the details. Perfectionism doesn't have much to do with sanctity.

It is important also to know well how to distinguish those cases where it is necessary to take time to discern and to decide, when it is a matter of decisions, for example, that affect our entire lives and the opposite cases where it would be stupid and contrary to the will of God to take too much time and too many precautions before deciding, when there is not much difference between one choice and another. As Saint Francis de Sales said, "If it is normal to weigh gold ingots with care, when it comes to small coins it is enough to make a quick evaluation." The devil, who is always seeking to disturb us, makes us ask ourselves, even in making the smallest decision, whether it is truly the will of the Lord or not to do thus and who creates unease, scruples and remorse of conscience for things that really aren't worth the trouble.

We must have a constant and profound desire to obey God. But this desire will be truly in accord with the Holy Spirit if it is accompanied by peace, interior freedom, confidence and abandonment and not if it is a source of trouble which paralyzes the conscience and prevents one from deciding freely.

It is true that the Lord can permit moments where this desire to obey Him causes real torment. There is also the case of persons who are scrupulous by temperament; this is a very painful trial from which the Lord never totally delivers them in this life.

But, it is still true that normally we must strive to advance along our path in such a fashion, in internal freedom and peace. And to know, as we have just said, that the devil tries passionately to trouble us. He is crafty and uses the desire we have to do God's will to disturb us. One must not let him "take advantage" of us. When one is far from God, the adversary tempts him with evil: he attracts him to bad things. But when one is close to God, loves Him, desires nothing but to please and obey Him, the devil, while he tempts him still with evil (this is easy to recognize), he tempts him even further by good. This means that he makes use of our desire to do good to trouble us. He does this by making us scrupulous, or by presenting us with a certain good that we must realize but which is beyond our present strength, or which is not what God asks of us — all to discourage us or to cause us to lose our peace. He wants to convince us that we are not doing enough or that what we are doing we are not really doing for the love of God, or that the Lord is not happy with us, etc. He would make us believe, for instance, that the Lord is asking such and such a sacrifice of us that we are incapable of doing, and this will trouble us greatly. It creates all sorts of scruples and worries in the conscience which we should purely and simply ignore, while throwing ourselves into the arms of God like small children. When we lose peace for reasons similar to those we just mentioned, let us tell ourselves that the devil must be involved. Let's try to regain our calm and, if we cannot do it by ourselves, we should open up to a spiritual person. The mere fact of speaking to another person will generally be enough to make our confusion disappear completely and to bring back our peace.

Regarding this spirit of freedom that should

animate us in all our actions and decisions, let us conclude by listening to Saint Francis de Sales:

> Keep your heart open and always in the hands of Divine Providence, whether for great things or small, and obtain for your heart more and more the spirit of gentleness and tranquility. (Letter to Mme. de la Fléchère, 13 May 1609)

> The word that I spoke to you so often was that you should not be too particular in the exercise of virtues, rather that you should pursue them briskly, openly, naively, in an old-fashioned way, with liberty, sincerity and *grosso modo*. It is because I fear the spirit of constraint and melancholy. It is my wish that you should have a large and open heart on the way to our Lord. (Letter to Mme. de Chantal, 1 November 1604)

17. The Royal Way of Love

All things considered, this manner of going forward, based on peace, liberty, confident abandonment to God, quiet acceptance of our shortcomings and even of our failures, why is this the way to counsel? Why is it more correct than seeking the will of God, which is done with preoccupation, scruples and a tense and restless desire for perfection?

Because **the only true perfection is that of love** and, in the first way of proceeding, there is more true love of God than in the second. Saint Faustina said: "When I do not know what to do, I question love, for love is the best counselor!" The Lord calls us to perfection: *Be perfect as your Father in heaven is perfect.* But still, according to the Bible, the one who is most perfect is not the one who behaves in an irreproachable manner, but the one who loves most.

The behavior that is most perfect is not that which corresponds to the image that we sometimes form for ourselves of perfection, such as a comportment that is impeccable, infallible and spotless. Rather, it is one where there is the most disinterested love of God and the least prideful pursuit of oneself. One who accepts to be weak, small and who fails often, who accepts to be nothing in his own eyes or in the eyes of others, but who, without being excessively preoccupied with his situation, because he is animated by a great confidence in God and knows that his love is infinitely more important and counts ever so much more than his own imperfections and faults, this person loves more than one who pushes the preoccupation of his own perfection to the point of anxiety.

Happy are the poor in spirit for the Kingdom of God is theirs. Happy are they, enlightened by the

Holy Spirit, who have learned to no longer make a drama of their poverty, but who accept it joyously because they put all their hope, not in themselves, but in God. God Himself will be their wealth, He will be their perfection, their sanctity, their virtues. Happy are those who know how to love their poverty, because it is a marvelous opportunity for God to manifest the immensity of His Love and His Mercy. We will be saints the day when our inabilities and our nothingness will no longer be for us a subject of sadness and anxiety, but a subject of peace and joy.

This road of poverty, which is also the way of love, is the most efficacious for making us grow, for making us progressively acquire all of the virtues, for purifying us of our faults. Love alone is the source of growth, it alone is fruitful, love alone purifies sin in depth: "The fire of love purifies more than the fires of purgatory," Saint Thérèse of Lisieux tells us. This approach, based on the joyous acceptance of one's own poverty is in no way equivalent to a resignation to mediocrity or an abdication of aspiring to perfection. Rather, it is the quickest and surest road to perfection because it puts us in the position of smallness, confidence and abandonment by which we are placed entirely in the hands of God Who can act in us by His grace and carry us Himself by pure mercy to the perfection that we, in no way, could achieve by our own strength.

18. Some Advice in the Guise of a Conclusion

Let us then seek to put into practice all that has been said, with patience and perseverance, and, above all, without becoming discouraged if we don't arrive at perfection! Permit me to formulate an axiom that is a little paradoxical: Above all we must never lose our peace because we can never find or be as much at peace as we would like! Our reeducation is long and it is necessary to have a lot of patience with ourselves.

This, then, is the fundamental principle: "I will never become discouraged!" This is another phrase taken from the little Thérèse, who is the consummate model of the spirit that we have attempted to describe in these pages. And let us also repeat the words of the great Saint Teresa of Avila, "Patience obtains everything."

Another very useful, practical principle is the following: If I am not capable of great things, I will not become discouraged, but I will do the small things! Sometimes, because we are unable to do great things, heroic acts, we neglect the small things that are available to us and which are, moreover, so fruitful for our spiritual progress and are such a source of joy: *Well done, good and faithful servant! You have been faithful over a few things, I will now trust you with greater. Come and share your master's joy* (Matthew 25:21). If the Lord finds us faithful and persevering in small things in terms of what He expects of us, it is He Himself who will intervene and establish us in a higher grace. The application: If I am still not able to remain at peace when faced with difficult situations, then it is better that I should begin to strive to keep this peace in the easier situations of everyday life: to quietly and without irritability do my daily chores, to commit myself to doing each thing well in the present moment without preoccupying myself with what follows, to speak peacefully and with gentleness to those around me, to avoid excessive hurry in my gestures and in the way I climb the stairs! The first steps on the ladder of sanctity could very well be those of my own apartment! The soul often is reeducated by the body! Small things done with love and to please God are extremely beneficial in making us grow; it's one of the secrets of holiness of Saint Thérèse of Lisieux.

And if we persevere in such a way, in prayer and with these small acts of collaboration with grace, we will be able to live the words of Saint Paul:

> *Don't be anxious; instead, give thanks in all your prayers and petitions and make your requests known to God. And God's peace which is beyond all understanding will keep your hearts and minds in Christ Jesus.* (Philippians 4:6-7)

And this peace nobody can take from us.

Part Three

What The Saints Tell Us

JUAN DE BONILLA

Spanish Franciscan of the 16th century,
author of a splendid little treatise on peace of soul.

1. Peace, the Road to Perfection

Experience shows us that peace, which sows charity, the love of God and love of neighbor in your soul, is the road that leads straight to eternal life.

Take care to never let your heart be troubled, saddened, agitated or involved in that which can cause it to lose its peace. Rather work always to remain tranquil because the Lord says: "Happy are those who are at peace." Do this and the Lord will build in your soul the City of Peace and He will make of you a House of Delight. That which He wants of you is that, whenever you are troubled, you would recover your calm, your peace, on your own — in your work, in your thoughts and in all your activities without exception.

Just as a city is not built in a day, do not think that you can achieve, in a day, this peace, this interior calm, because it is within you that a home must be built for God, while you yourself, become His temple. And it is the Lord Himself Who must handle the construction. Without Him your work would not exist.

Remind yourself, moreover, that this edifice has humility for its foundation.

2. Maintain a Free and Detached Soul

Your will should always be ready for every eventuality. And your heart must not be enslaved by anything. When you form some desire, it should not be such as to cause you to experience pain in case of failure, but you should keep your spirit as tranquil as though you had never wished for anything. True freedom consists in not being attached to anything. It is in this detachment that God seeks your soul in order to work His great marvels.[1]

---

[1] This passage was translated directly from the French editions, *Traité de la paix des âmes* (*A Treatise on the Peace of Souls*), Juan de Bonilla, Editions Notre Dame de la Trinité, Blois, 1964, and *La paix intérieure* (*Interior Peace*), Juan de Bonilla, Editions Lion de Juda, 1991.

FRANCIS DE SALES
(1567-1622)

1. God is the God of Peace

Because love only resides in peace, always be careful to conserve the holy tranquility of heart that I have so often recommended to you.

None of the thoughts that render us anxious and agitated in spirit in any way comes from God, Who is the Prince of Peace. These are the temptations of the enemy and consequently one must reject them and not take them into account.

One must everywhere and in everything live peacefully. If pain comes to us, whether internally or exteriorly, one must receive it peacefully. If joy should come to us, one must receive it peacefully, without wincing because of it. Must one run from evil? It must be done peacefully, without being troubled, otherwise, in fleeing, we could fall and give the enemy the leisure to do us in. If one must do good, one must do it peacefully, otherwise we will commit many faults in our eagerness. Even in matters of penance, one must do it peacefully. (Letter to the Abbess du Puy d'Orbe)

2. How to Obtain Peace

Let us do three things, my dearest daughter, and we will have peace: let us have the very pure intention of will to do all things for the honor and glory of God; let us do the little that we can toward that end, according to the advice of our spiritual director; and let us leave it to God to take care of all the rest. Why should anyone who has God for the object of his intentions and does whatever he can be troubled? Of what should he be afraid? No, no. God is not so terrible with those who love Him. He is content with very little because He knows well that we don't have much. And know, my dear daughter, that our Lord is called the Prince of Peace in Scripture and, consequently, everywhere where He is the absolute master, He maintains all things in peace. It is nevertheless true that before bringing peace to a given place, He makes war with it, separating the heart and the soul of the most loved, familiar and ordinary affections, that is to say, the exaggerated love of self, confidence in and complacency with oneself, and similar affections.

Now, when our Lord separates us from these passions, so sweet and so dear, it seems that He flays the heart alive and we experience very angry feelings; it's almost all we can do to struggle with all our soul, because this separation is strongly felt. But all this spiritual agitation is, however, not without peace, as, finally, overwhelmed by this distress, we neither fail for this reason to conform our will to our Lord's will and to maintain it there, riveted to this divine pleasure, nor do we abandon by any means our duties and their accomplishment; rather, we carry them out courageously. (Letter to the Abbess du Puy d'Orbe)

3. Peace and Humility

Peace is born of humility.

Nothing troubles us but pride and the esteem that we have for ourselves. What does it tell us if we should experience some imperfection or sin, and find that we are surprised, troubled and impatient? Without doubt, it is that we think ourselves to be something good, resolute and solid; and, consequently, when we see, effectively, that none of this is true and that we have had our heads in the sand, that we were mistaken, as a consequence, we feel troubled, offended and ill at ease. If we knew ourselves well, rather than being flabbergasted to find ourselves on the ground, we would wonder how we manage to remain standing.

4. All Things Contribute to the Good of Those Who Love God

All things contribute to good for those who love God. And, as a matter of fact, since God can and does know how to draw good from evil, for whom should He do it, if not for those who, without reserve, have given themselves to Him?

Yes, even sins, from which God by His goodness defends us, are reduced by Divine Providence to good for those who belong to Him. Never would David have been so full of humility had he not sinned, nor would Mary Magdelene have been so full of love for her Lord if He had not remitted so many of her sins. And never could He have forgiven her these sins if she had not committed them.

You see, my daughter, this great architect of mercy: He converts our miseries into grace and makes salutary medicine for our souls from the venom of our iniquities.

Tell me, please, what could He not do with our afflictions, our sufferings and the persecutions that we endure? If, then, you are ever touched by some unpleasantness, from wherever it may come, assure your soul that, if it loves God, everything will be converted to good. And although you may not see the means by which this good will happen to you, be assured that it will happen. If God allows your eyes to be blinded by the mud of ignominy, it is to give you a clear vision as a way of honoring you. If God makes you fall, as He did with Saint Paul, whom He threw to the ground, it is to raise you up to His glory.

5. One Should Absolutely Desire God Alone, the Rest in Moderation

One should only want God absolutely, invariably and inviolably; but, regarding the means of serving Him, one should only desire them slowly and gently, so that if we are prevented from using them, we would not be greatly upset.

6. Trust in Providence

The measure of Divine Providence in us depends on the degree of trust that we have in it.

Do not anticipate the unpleasant events of this life by apprehension, rather anticipate them with the perfect hope that, as they happen, God, to Whom you belong, will protect you. He has protected you up to the present moment; just remain firmly in the hands of His providence and He will help you in all situations and at those times when you find yourself unable to walk, He will carry you. What should you fear, my dearest daughter, since you belong to God Who has so strongly assured us that for those who love Him all things turn into happiness. Do not think of what may happen tomorrow, because the same eternal Father Who takes care of you today, will take care of you tomorrow and forever. Either He will see that nothing bad happens to you or, if He allows anything bad to happen to you, He will give you the invincible courage to bear it.

Remain at peace, my daughter. Remove from your imagination whatever may upset you and say frequently to our Lord, "O God, You are my God and I will trust in You; You will help me and You will be my refuge and there is nothing I will fear, because not only are You with me, but, also, You are in me and I in You." What does a child in the arms of such a Father have to fear? Be as a little child, my dearest daughter. As you know, children don't concern themselves with many matters; they have others who think for them. They are strong enough if they remain with their father. Therefore, act accordingly, my daughter, and you will be at peace.

7. One Should Avoid Haste

You should treat your affairs with care, but never with hurry or worry.

Don't rush to your tasks, because any haste upsets your reason and judgment and even prevents you from doing well the very thing that you are hurrying to do....

When our Lord reprimanded Saint Martha, He said to her: *"Martha, Martha, you are anxious and upset over many things."* You see, if she had simply been caring, she would hardly have been troubled; but because she was worried and anxious, she becomes hurried and upset. And this is why our Lord reprimanded her....

Never is a task accomplished with impetuosity and haste done well.... Therefore, accept with peace all the tasks that come to you and try to accomplish them in order, one after the other.

8. Peace When Confronted by Our Faults

We must hate our shortcomings, but with a hate that is tranquil and peaceful, not with a hate that is fretful and troubled; and, yes, we must have the patience to see our shortcomings and to profit from a saintly abasement of ourselves. Failing that, my daughter, your imperfections, which you see very acutely, will trouble you even more keenly, and, by this means maintain themselves, as there is nothing which sustains our defects more than a sense of anxiety and haste to eliminate them.

9. Gentleness and Peace in One's Zeal Towards Others

O my daughter, God has granted you a great mercy to have recalled your heart to the gracious support of others and to have poured the holy balm of sweetness of heart toward your fellow man into the wine of your zeal.

That's all that you needed, my dearest daughter; your zeal was altogether good, but it had the defect of being a little harsh, a bit too urgent, a bit anxious and irritable. Now, it has been purified of these things; from now on it will be gentle, kind, gracious, peaceful and enduring. (Letter to a Mistress of Novices)

10. And Finally: Accepting, Without Becoming Troubled, Not Always Being Able to Maintain One's Peace

Strive, my daughter, to maintain your heart at peace by being even-tempered. I don't say maintain your heart at peace, but I say strive to do so. This should be your main concern. And beware of occasions for troubling yourself, because you cannot moderate so suddenly the ups and downs of your feelings.[2]

---

[2] These passages were translated directly from the French *Oeuvres Complètes*, published by the Visitation d'Annecy. An English language version can be found in the book *Serenity of Heart: Bearing the Troubles of This Life*, Sophia Institute Press, 1997.

TERESA OF AVILA
(1515-1582)

Genuine and False Humility

Let us beware also, my daughters, of certain forms of humility that are suggested by the devil. He throws us into the most lively disquietude by depicting the gravity of our sins. This is one of the areas where he troubles souls in many ways.... Everything these souls do seems to be surrounded by danger; all their good deeds, as good as they may be, seem unuseful to them. Such discouragement causes them to give up, they feel powerless to accomplish any good, because they imagine that everything that is praiseworthy in others is bad in themselves.

Humility, as great as it may be, does not disquiet, trouble or agitate the soul; it is rather accompanied by peace, joy and repose. Without doubt, awareness of misery clearly shows the soul that it merits hell and plunges it into affliction; it appears to the soul that all other creatures must view it with horror, and justly so; the soul does not dare, in a manner of speaking, ask for mercy. But when humility is genuine, this pain fills the soul with such sweetness and contentment that the soul would not like to be deprived of it; it does not trouble the soul and hardly constricts it; rather, on the contrary, it enlarges it and makes it better able to serve God. This has nothing in common with the other type of pain, which upsets all things, agitates everything, completely disturbs the soul and is full of anger. In my opinion, the devil would like us to believe that we possess humility and, if he could, he would like to cause us, in exchange, to lose all confidence in God. (*Way of Perfection*, Chapter 41)[3]

---

[3] This passage was translated directly from the French *Oeuvres Complètes*, tr. by Fr. G. de Saint-Joseph, Seuil. An English language version can be found in the book *Way of Perfection*, tr. by E. Allison Peers, New York: Doubleday, 1991.

MARIE OF THE INCARNATION
(1566-1618)

Abandonment to God's Will

If we could, with a single interior glance, see all the goodness and mercy that exists in God's designs for each one of us, even in what we call disgraces, pains and afflictions, our happiness would consist in throwing ourselves into the arms of the Divine Will, with the abandon of a young child that throws himself into the arms of his mother. We would behave, in all things, with the intention of pleasing God and then we would maintain ourselves in a holy repose, fully convinced that God is our Father and that He desires our salvation more than we ourselves desire it.

FRANÇOIS-MARIE-JACOB LIBERMANN
(1802-1852)

A converted Jew, founder of the Fathers of the Holy
Spirit. Extracts of letters of spiritual direction.

1. Peace: The Reign of Jesus in the Soul

The best ways to establish in ourselves the
admirable reign of Jesus are precisely those of continual prayer and peace of soul....

Remind yourself of this constantly and
strongly establish this truth in your spirit and in your
heart that the best way, and even the infallible way,
of being in continual prayer is to keep one's soul at
peace before the Lord.

Pay attention to these words: "Keep your soul
at peace." It is an expression employed by our Divine Master. Your soul should always be enclosed
in itself — or better enclosed in Jesus Who dwells
therein — not imprisoned or locked up under key,
but in gentle repose, kept in Jesus, Who holds it in
His arms.

Effort and contention constrict the soul, but
a gentle repose, a peaceful manner of behaving and
a steady, measured and quiet interior action expand
it.

2. Peace, a Condition for Docility of Spirit

Our souls, shaken and tormented by their own forces, tossed to and fro, right and left, cannot allow themselves to belong to the Spirit of God. They would find their strength, their richness and all their perfection in the Spirit of our Lord, if only they were willing to abandon themselves to His guidance. But, because they leave the Spirit of our Lord and want to act by themselves and in themselves, they only find in themselves trouble, misery and the deepest powerlessness... We should aim for this peace and this inner moderation, with a view to living only in God and through God, in all sweetness and submission, and striving steadfastly to renounce ourselves. One must forget oneself in order to continually direct one's soul toward God and keep it gently and quietly before Him.

3. Confidence in God

I would like to be able to strongly reprimand you for having so little confidence in our Lord. You should not fear Him, this greatly offends Him Who is so good, so sweet, so kind and so full of tenderness and mercy toward us. You may stand before Him in complete embarrassment because of your poverty and abjectness, but this embarrassment should be that of the prodigal son, after his return

— confident and full of tenderness. This is the way you should appear before Jesus, our good Father and Lord. You are still in fear of not loving Him. It is more likely, in these moments, my dearest, that you love Him the most and that He is closer to you than ever. Don't measure your love of our Lord by the depth of your feelings; this is truly a small measure. Abandon yourself into His hands with confidence; your love will increase more and more, but you will not notice it, and that does not matter.

4. Don't Let Your Misfortune Upset You

Don't ever allow yourself to become upset by your misfortunes. In face of your misery, should you find yourself in this situation by the will of God, remain humble and lowly before God and be at great peace. Respond to all misfortune, whatever it may be, with gentleness, peace, tenderness and interior moderation before God, abandoning yourself simply into His hands so that He may make of you and in you what He pleases. Wish calmly and peacefully to live only for Him, through Him and in Him.

5. Don't Let Your Apparent Lukewarmness Upset You

Don't allow yourself to become disheartened or discouraged if it appears that you are making no progress, if you are fainthearted and lukewarm, if you should see that you are still subject to natural affections, thoughts of pride and sad feelings. Simply strive to forget all these things and turn your mind toward God, standing before Him in the quiet and continuous desire that He make of you and in you His holy pleasure. Aim only at forgetting yourself and at walking before Him in the midst of your poverty, without ever looking at yourself… As long as you are concerned with the capriciousness of nature, you will be busy with yourself and, as long as you are busy with yourself, you will not make much progress on the way to perfection. These capricious movements will stop only when you hold them in contempt and forget them. Besides, I assure you that they are of no importance nor of any consequence; don't pay any attention to them, only look at God and this with a pure and simple faith.

6. Don't Worry About Your Falls

Always forget the past and never worry about your falls, many as they may be. So long as you get back on your feet, no harm will have been done;

whereas, a great deal of harm will occur if you lose heart or if you berate yourself too much for your failures. Do everything with the greatest possible calm and serenity and out of the greatest, purest and holiest love of Jesus and Mary.

7. Patience

One of the principal obstacles one encounters on the way to perfection is the precipitous and impatient desire to progress and to possess those virtues that we feel we don't have. On the contrary, the true means of solidly advancing, and with giant steps, is to be patient and to calm and pacify these anxieties.... Don't get ahead of your guide for fear of getting lost and straying from the path that He indicates, because, if you do, instead of arriving safe and sound, you will fall into a pit. Your guide is the Holy Spirit. By your struggles and worries, by your anxiety and haste, you overtake Him with the pretense of moving more quickly. And then what happens? You stray from the path and find yourself on terrain that is harder and rougher and, far from advancing, you go backwards; at a minimum, you waste your time.

8. Let the Spirit of God Act

When it pleased God to create the universe, He worked with nothing, and look at the beautiful things He made! In the same way, if He wants to work in us to accomplish things infinitely beyond all the natural beauties which came from His hands, He doesn't need our becoming so agitated to help Him.... Rather, let Him work by Himself; He likes to work with nothingness. Let us stay peacefully and quietly before Him and simply follow the changes that He produces.... Let us then keep our souls at peace and our spiritual forces at rest before Him, while awaiting every motion and sign of life from Him alone. And let us endeavor not to move, will or live, except in God and through the Spirit of God. It is necessary to forget oneself and continually direct one's soul toward God and leave it calmly and peacefully before Him.

9. Moderating One's Desires

The main occupation of your soul should be to moderate its movements and to acquire a humble attitude of submission and abandonment into the hands of God. You are allowed, it is even good, to desire your spiritual advancement, but this desire must be calm, humble and submissive to the will of God. A poor beggar, who begs insistently makes people impatient and gets nothing. If he begs humbly, with gentleness and kindness, he touches those from whom he is begging. Excessively insistent desires come from nature. Everything that comes from grace is gentle, humble, and moderate; it fills the soul and makes it good and submissive to God. Your particular effort should therefore consist in moderating the movements of your soul, keeping it calm, submissive and humble before God.

You wish to progress on the way to holiness; it is He Who gives you this desire and it is also He Who must accomplish it. Saint Paul says that it is God Who makes us want and do. We cannot want anything in the realm of grace by ourselves. It is God Who gives us this desire. When we have it, we cannot bring it to fulfillment by ourselves. God gives us the means. Our role is to be faithful in following God's lead, leaving Him to do in us what seems best to Him. To worry, to hurry in carrying out the good desires that He inspires in us is to spoil the work of grace in us and to draw us away from our perfection. Let us not try to be perfect immediately; let us undertake our accomplishments with calm, with a peaceful fidelity to that which He demands of us. If it pleases Him to move our boat more gently than we should desire, let us be submissive to His divine will.

When we always see the same faults in ourselves, let us remain in our lowliness before Him. Let us open our souls to Him so that He may see our wounds and our scars that it may please Him to heal us when and as He desires. Very simply, let us try not to follow the impulse of these faults. And in that regard, let us employ, as our only means, keeping ourselves prostrate humbly before Him with our poverty and misery in full view, enduring the onset of our faults with calm, patience, gentleness, confidence and humility before God, keenly determined to be everything to Him in spite of our faults, and not to give in to them but to endure them until the end of our lives, if such is His will. Because, mark this well, once our souls refuse to consent to these faults, they are no longer culpable, God is no longer offended and, on the contrary, our souls will profit greatly for their advancement.

10. Living in the Present Instant

Be docile and pliable in the hands of God. You know what you must do to achieve this. Keep yourself at peace and in complete repose, never become upset and never trouble yourself about anything, forget the past, live as though the future does not exist, live for Jesus in every moment that you are living, or, better, live as though you have no life in yourself, but allow Jesus to live in you at His leisure; to walk thus, in all circumstances and in all encounters, without fear or worry as is becoming the children of Jesus and Mary; never think of yourself voluntarily; abandon the care of your soul to Jesus alone, etc. It is He who takes the soul by force; it belongs to Him. It is therefore up to Him to take care of it because it is His property. Do not fear so much the judgment of such a tender Master. Generally speaking, banish all fear and replace this feeling with love; in all of this, act gently, sweetly, steadily, without haste, without anger. Act as if you were dead when the need is there. Walk in this fashion in all graciousness, abandonment and complete confidence. The time of this exile will end and Jesus will belong to us and we to Him. Then each of our tribulations will be a crown of glory for us that we will place on the head of Jesus, because all glory is His alone.

11. Our Incapacities: A Subject Not of Sadness and Distress, but One of Peace and Joy

The sight of our incapacities and our nothingness should be for us a great subject of peace, by convincing us that God Himself wishes to operate in us and through us to accomplish all the wonderful things for which He has destined us, because He knows ever so much better than we our poverty and our misery. Why, then, has He chosen us, knowing that we can do nothing, if not to demonstrate, with evidence, that it is He Who will do the work and not we?

But a subject of still greater joy, it seems to me, is that our extreme misery and ignominy place us in the absolute necessity of always having recourse to our God and keeping closely united with Him at every moment and in all the circumstances of our lives. We depend on Him more than our bodies depend on our souls. Is it troublesome, I ask, for our bodies to be in continual dependence on our souls and to receive from the soul all life and movement? On the contrary, this is the very glory of the body and highly agreeable to it because it thereby becomes a participant in a life that is much more noble and elevated that it would have by itself. The same thing is true with regard to our dependence on God, but in a far superior way. The more we are dependent on Him, the more our souls acquire grandeur, beauty and glory, so much so that we can heartily glory in our infirmities. The greater our infirmities, the greater, too, our joy and happiness, because our dependence on God becomes that much more necessary. Thus, then, my dear son, do not be disturbed any longer if you feel yourself weak. On the contrary, rejoice, because God will be your strength. Only take care to keep your soul ever turned towards Him in the greatest possible peace, the most perfect abandonment and the greatest embarrassment and humiliation of yourself.[4]

---

[4] This passage was translated directly from the French edition of *Lettres du Vénérable Père Libermann* (Letters of the Venerable Father Libermann), compiled by L. Vogel, DDB, Paris, 1964.

PADRE PIO
1887-1968

Capuchin priest and stigmatist, canonized by
Pope John Paul II on June 16, 2002.

Peace is the simplicity of spirit, the serenity
of conscience, the tranquility of the soul and the
bond of love. Peace is order, it is the harmony in
each one of us, it is a continual joy that is born in
witnessing a clear conscience, it is the holy joy of a
heart wherein God reigns. Peace is the way to perfection, or, even better, in peace dwells perfection.
And the devil, who knows all this very well, does
everything possible to cause us to lose our peace.
The soul need be saddened by only one thing: an
offense against God. But even on this point, one
must be very prudent. One must certainly regret
one's failures, but with a peaceful sorrow and always
trusting in Divine Mercy. One must beware of certain reproaches and remorse against oneself which
most of the time come from our enemy who wants
to disturb our peace in God. If such reproaches and
remorse humble us and make us quick to do the
right thing, without taking away our confidence in
God, we may be assured that they come from God.
However, if they confuse us and make us fearful,

distrustful, lazy or slow to do the right thing, we may be sure that they come from the devil and we should consequently push them aside, finding our refuge in confidence in God.